Myth and
Christian Belief

Myth and Christian Belief

William J. Duggan

FIDES PUBLISHERS, INC.
NOTRE DAME, INDIANA

© Copyright: 1971, Fides Publishers, Inc.
Notre Dame, Indiana

LCCCN: 76-140145
ISBN: 0-8190-0431-6

To Danny

Contents

Acknowledgements

This book would not have taken shape were it not for the engaging questions of my students. I am indebted to the students at Webster College for my own growth. I would like to express my appreciation to my wife, Barbara, who assisted greatly in the many revisions of the manuscript. I want to thank Tom and Pam Linehan for their constant encouragement. The drawings and charts were done by Pam Linehan. Finally, I would like to thank Adelaide Whitesitt whose editing suggestions were invaluable.

Introduction

Life is lived today within the context of revolution. The gradual steps of evolution have given way to the leaps and bounds along the path of history. Science, technology, and society form the inner core of the swirling cosmic cell centrifugally creative of revolution, each in its own nucleus. Science has shot us far out into space and far into the depths of the human body so that moon-walking and heart transplants dazzle our imagination and smash images of man and his world of yesteryear. Technology has made the leap from horsepower to speed of sound. The pace of life has intensified the business of survival. Near-missed jets, air-polluting autos, deadening lakes, population explosions, trees displaced by bricks, are setting the human species on a collision course. The cool medium of television unnoticeably continues to shape and mold the conscience of society. This whimsical one-eyed monster displaces divine revelation spewing forth its on-the-spot coverage of every aspect of human existence. The T.V. mis-information machine is creating a half-informed and divided society. The haves and have-nots, intellectually as well as materially, are lining up in preparation for a confrontation in the great society. A great satire on technology

1

has already been acted out with the striking of matches to the cities as symbolic candles, lighting the darkness.

In this time of revolution which touches so many areas in our lives, can religion walk with its head high in the clouds of security pretending that the chaos is just a passing phase displayed by man, a spoiled child? The college classroom of religion says otherwise. The revolution has broken into the sanctum of religious security. Faith convictions previously ghettoed deeply within the psyche are forced to bear the impact of social and cultural pressures. The college class has ceased to be a group of recipient students jotting down incipient lectures. The silence is pierced with question after question. Courses in religion multiply to meet the searching needs of the students. The phenomenon is taking place on the campuses of state and private colleges and universities alike. The college class of religion is a mirror of the growing unrest of generations of men and women. The questions are not vague. They are direct, arising out of the depths of the student's personality in conflict with his inherited convictions. They are not questions of morality, but are fundamental questions concerning the nature of man and his relationship to God and to his fellow man. The questions are raised as challenges of life experience as against inherited faith experience. The student drives home the point that there is a credibility gap between contemporary living and traditional believing. Yet, out-dated language continues to attempt communication from established pulpits.

In the religion classes of colleges it is the students who are raising the questions, not the instructors. The

role of the instructor has changed from the denomina-
tional indoctrinator to the center-fielder of the hard-
hitting questions. Canned answers to the questions of
students result in a very fast and effective turn-off. Our
society is largely of a Judaic-Christian background. This
background manifests a rich variety of expression. The
pluralism of faith creates a dynamic atmosphere of
honesty and respect as students of different faiths struggle with each others' faith questions. These faith questions also come from the atheist and the agnostic as well
as from the believing student. To be caught up in the
ebullient exchanges of varied beliefs is an enriching experience. The atmosphere is one of search and struggle,
not one of hostility, although at times facing one's religious beliefs is productive of defense mechanisms. This
book concerns itself with the problem areas of today's
students. The effort is addressed to the students of
Judaic-Christian traditions, but not to the exclusion of
the agnostic or the atheist. However, effort has no guar-
antee of truth. This book is not concerned with definitive alternatives, but with the creation of respect for
the wide range of religious struggles of today's college
generation.

The direction we pursue reflects the questions raised
by the students, and concerns the origin of man and the
origin of man's religious thought. The questions do not
rest merely with origins. Ultimately, the problem is how
to *talk* about traditional Judaic-Christian beliefs in contemporary language. The challenge is to re-express basic
faith formulations yet with fidelity to the traditions.
Specifically, this book will concern itself with the questions about the origins of the cosmos, the origins of man,

his sinfulness, his redemption, the resurrection and the after-life. We hope to establish the relation between the primitive expressions of religious belief and classical Christian formulations. Drawing upon biblical research and biological evolution, we intend to recast basic Judaic-Christian beliefs. The new expressions are alternatives which themselves remain open to the data of the future. Adhering to the Judaic-Christian idea will create the paradox of descriptions in contemporary language as against the sacrosanct language of the past. The resolution of the seeming contradictions rests on the principle that no matter what man says about God or about what God has *said*, will, in the last analysis, find its expression in human language.

The first chapter is a brief statement of the thesis, the purpose, and the challenge of this book. The paradox lies precisely in the problem of faith as an acquisition against faith as a search. Is faith past oriented or future oriented? A solution to this problem lies buried within the very concept of revelation.

The second chapter of this book concerns itself with the language of mythology. It then describes the function of mythology and its relation to the Old and New Testaments. It establishes the difficulty of humanly expressing the mystery of God's presence. The problem within Christian mythological language is the hellenistic tendency to elevate symbolic description to the level of historical event. An outstanding example of this is found in the elevation of the symbolic Genesis description of man's sinfulness in terms of original sin to the level of an actual event in the history of man, including all the details of Adam, Eve, apple, snake, and fig leaf.

The third chapter applies the clarification of myth to the origin of the world, pointing out the varied creation stories of biblical times and suggesting that the Hebrew story of creation draws upon symbols shared by other writers of that time. Christianity inherited the Creation Story from the Hebrew Old Testament but gradually doctrinal formulations filtered the mythology of the Old Testament through the prism of Greek philosophical thought. Symbolism gave way to historical fact. Contemporary man is dissatisfied with the classical descriptions of creation. Chapter Three is an attempt to re-express the origin of the world in terms more compatible with the biblical and scientific data available today.

The fourth chapter concerns itself with the creation of man. Primitive scriptures have rich and imaginative descriptions concerning the creation of man. The Old Testament shares in these descriptions. Christianity embellished the Old Testament concept of man's origin with its peculiarly Greek description of man's nature. Can we speak about man today in terms different from the classical Christian description and remain faithful to the biblical faith of man's image of God?

Chapter five deals with the problem of evil in the human community and its re-expression in language other than that of the Original Sin myth. Human existence and experience is pervaded with the mysteries of pain, suffering, death, tragedy, and other manifestations of evil. The fifth chapter discusses the problem of evil as described by the Babylonians and Hebrews. It then changes the classical original sin formulations into a different consideration of the problem of man's sinfulness.

The following two chapters elaborate on man's mythmaking. The Flood Story and Call of Abraham and Moses are rich with the symbols of Middle Eastern religious thinking. The "calls" of Abraham, Moses and Jesus are placed in similar psychological patterns of response to God within the context of tragedies of the people.

The seventh chapter concerns itself with the Christian Incarnation. The classical description of Jesus and his relationship to God expressed in the New Testament is expressed in the language forms of his times. Jesus was effectively and meaningfully preached throughout the Roman-Greco world because Persian, Greek, and Hebrew religious frameworks had conditioned the people of these times to accept one such as Jesus, particularly in terms of his divine relationship to God. One of the fundamental problems facing Christianity today is preaching Jesus in meaningful language to a people far removed from New Testament times. A further but related problem, is the dusting over of the original Jesus documents with centuries of cultural interpretations. In the last analysis, the description of Jesus as outlined in the seventh chapter is a cultural interpretation. The Christian tragedy has been that one or another cultural interpretation of Jesus has been served up as the *only* possible language form in which to speak the mystery of Jesus.

The next chapter takes up the question of the Resurrection. It remains one of the chief areas of questioning by the college student. The problem centers not so much on what later Christianity interpreted as Resurrection, but on what the New Testament writers wrote of the Resurrection. This is no small task. We can, however, speak about the primitive resurrection myths, which, by way of a very complex route, found their way into a unified description of the Resurrection of Jesus. The question is whether we can speak about the resurrection in quite different language frameworks and yet remain faithful to the basic Christian belief concerning man's final glory.

Resurrection is a resurrection to the afterlife. Because it is so related to the question of resurrection, new expressions of the afterlife are in order. It is not a definitive alternative, but rather a prognosis more consistent with the human experience of death than the present Christian one. In re-expressing the mystery of the afterlife, there is the same procedure and right as exercised by the writers of the Old and New Testaments, the later Fathers, the great Councils, and less distinguished religious thinkers . . . the struggle and the search for meaningful language in which to dress the mysteries of God. Our generation has the task of re-expressing Christian beliefs, but in so doing, we are doing no more than what has constituted the history of Christianity.

1. The Challenge

faith as a search and not an acquisition · a commitment to understanding and not a list of truths · religious language and human experience · biblical expressions reflect a primitive culture · the problem of language in expressing religious mystery

My thesis is simple. Religious belief is a dynamic element of human life, now in the process of change. We cannot live in this world of constant change and expect our religious beliefs to remain untouched. Yet, this is what we have been taught to expect. It is this subtle and persistent expectation that creates the tension deep within us as we are torn between the experience of constant change and the desire for stable religious belief. The stability of religious faith has been served up to us as the wonder-rod of security in a world run wild.

My purpose is equally simple, to find a means of explaining religious faith in keeping with life as it is lived today. Many Christians are uncomfortable in what seems to be Christianity run wild. Christian periodicals have multiplied, submerging the community with many new and often strange interpretations of the Gospels. Theologians utter cliches that bounce off our ears as blasphemies. The "God-is-Dead" group is a relevant example. Their words did not mean what they seemed to say. For some, it meant that the word "God", dusted over with centuries of cultural nuances, has passed into oblivion.[1] For others, the God of the Hebrews died in the symbol of Jesus only to be resurrected in the activity of the Spirit.[2] This is not a criticism of the "God-is-Dead" theologians. Rather, it serves to point out the limitations and confusion of language used to convey inner convictions.

The challenge to which we address ourselves lies in the conviction, on one hand, that belief is *not* a commitment of a list of humanly-formulated absolute truths, but a constant search for self-meaning and understanding.[3] In this struggle, the reality of God is discovered and rediscovered. Faith is basically a search, not an acquisition. On the other hand, faith demands fidelity and sensitivity to the evolution of Christian traditions.[4] The solution lies in the recognition of God's revelation and man's interpretation of that revelation, as evolutional, unfolding within the evolution of man himself.

To the believer, God is a living reality who, down through the ages, has communicated himself with man, and conversely, the many ways in which man has, down through the ages, *understood* this divine communication. Faith is the belief that God *is* and in some way has spoken his *Isness* to man. Theology gives interpretation and understanding to God's activity in man's world. The Old Testament, for example, is an entire epic of man's interpretation of God's activity in man's world. The same can be said of the New Testament. Testaments are witnesses to God's activity. Testaments are theologies giving expression to man's faith. Both the Old and New Testaments are human expressions or human theologies that express man's faith-convictions. But such human expressions are very old, having sprung from very ancient cultures that differ profoundly from that of twentieth-century man. Neither Jew nor Christian can afford the luxury of resting his search for God in the primitive Testaments popularly known as the Bible. This does not take away from the Bible its privileged role as the foundation book of Judaism and Christianity. But, neither Judaism nor Christianity can survive the modern revolutions unless testaments are uttered today in language that springs out of the experience of contemporary man.[5] The crisis in Christianity today is a crisis of theology and theology has a problem of language.[6] The challenge is to pass on to younger generations an understanding of all that the Bible means in language and faith expressions that will have relevance to life as it must be lived today. The Bible incorporates the foundational beliefs of Christianity. Unfortunately, there is much confusion concerning what is basic and what is historical addenda. Theology interprets God's presence in man's world. But, man's world is changing. Interpretation of God is necessarily caught up in the processes of change. This does not mean that God is changing in the sense of changeable essence. It does mean that the vehicles for revealing His presence are changing. Changing man and changing world offer constantly changing reflections or signs of God's activity.

Two academic disciplines necessitate a change in contemporary theology. These disciplines are biblical research and biological evolution. The choice of these two disciplines rests on their relationship to man's self-understanding in regard to his nature and in regard to his religious expression of that understanding. Each of these two fields has brought forth evidence that demands a change in the language of Christian faith. Biological evolution has thrown light on God's creation of matter and man, original sin, the meaning of Jesus, and the afterlife. Biblical research has shown that many of our cherished beliefs originate in primitive and ancient mythologies. The writings of the Scriptures are primitive. Their social structures were primitive. Their attitudes toward women were primitive. Their vehicles of travel were primitive. Biblical times were primitive times and the expressions of faith could be couched only in the terms that reflected the primitive cultures of both the Old and the New Testaments. The fact that we live in times vastly different from the times in which the foundations for Judaic-Christian faith were laid, makes it necessary to address ourselves to that faith in words and images that come out of our modern experience rather than the experience of those who lived almost two thousand years ago.[7] Our challenge is to *improve* upon the language of the Old and New Testaments in expressing our belief that God continues to act within the world of man. It is not a question of rejecting the fundamental truths of the Judaic-Christian faith, but a question of finding more adequate expressions of that faith.[8]

Evolution is not a new concept within the community

of man. Ancient Greek philosophers grappled with the problem of the origin of species. Some were explicit in their conviction that man evolved from lesser forms of matter. Nor was the idea of evolution foreign to early Greek-Christian thinkers. Augustine, Basil the Great, and Gregory of Nyssa believed in some form of evolution.[9] What *is* new today in the area of Christian theology is the synthesizing of biological evolution with traditional expressions of Christian belief. Such a synthesizing is necessary if Christianity is to remain a viable and credible expression of faith for the younger generations, ever more exposed to the biological data that substantiates the theory of evolution.

In 1960, a group of scientists held a convention at the University of Chicago in honor of Charles Darwin. The following definition of evolution resulted:

> Evolution is definable in general terms as a one-way irreversible process in time, which, during its course generated novelty, diversity, and higher levels of organization. It operates in all sectors of the phenomenal universe but has been most fully described and analyzed in the biological sector.[10]

Teilhard de Chardin insists that all areas of human experience, including philosophy and theology must bow to the forces of evolution.[11] Biological evolution can no longer be referred to simply as a mere hypothesis, since data has been accumulated to substantiate the proposition that present forms of life have come forth from previous and less complex forms of life, and that all living forms of organic life have come forth from the non-living elements.

Anthropologists, paleontologists, biologists, botanists, and comparative anatomists accept the framework of evolution. The driving force of evolution remains a mystery, perhaps because the driving force is so intimately related to the divine. Communities of Christians may still be reluctant to accept evolution. High school teachers of biology run shy of evolution in explanations concerning the forces of nature. We know this from the number of college students who come to us either with negative attitudes toward evolution or no knowledge of it at all. It is time the Christian communities came to terms with the fact that evolution and Christian belief are completely compatible. We believe, like John Robinson, that basic Christian beliefs not only survive, but are enriched by the fact of evolution.[12] The beliefs will have to be recast in the light of evolution, but this will be consistent with the history of theology. The shift in the Christian community was first from the New Testament world of Palestine to the theologizing by the Greek fathers. Our effort is to remove Christian theology from the language of the philosophers of the middle ages to the religious language of the twentieth century.

What then are some of the basic Christian beliefs, the re-expressions of which become necessary in recognizing the fact of evolution? First and foremost, the origin of the world and of man should be placed in the total perspective of evolution. The creation of the world and creation of man can no longer be looked upon as isolated acts of God, but as linear results of God's initial acts of creation bringing into existence the *other-than-Himself*. In individual chapters we will consider the creation of the world and the creation of man in detail. Furthermore, the biblical story of Adam and Eve and the Fall of Man will have to give way to facts of man's origin and his struggle for survival in terms other than the mythical tree of good and evil and the challenge of the snake. Let me assure the reader that the basic Christian belief of man's creation by God and his struggle with evil will remain intact, although described in language which we feel will speak to man's understanding in a way far more relevant than the expressions of Genesis.

Consequent to the re-expression of the Christian belief concerning original sin, will be the need to reconsider the role of Jesus as Redeemer. The redemptive value of Jesus as one who buys man back from the state of alienation, will give way to a Christ who constantly gives human existence a whole new thrust toward God. Redemption is more meaningful in the light of a new relationship with God rather than a buying man back from the forces of evil. Death will be seen in the terms of evolution as a transformation to a new level of existence, not as a violent interruption of the unity of body and soul due to man's sinfulness. The wages of sin is not death. Death is the natural result of worn out or destroyed cell structures. Resurrection is the breaking forth of the individual spirit of man into a new level of personal existence and experience. It will no longer be confined to the notion of final unity of body with soul. There is hardly any facet of Christian faith that will not undergo re-expression as Christianity identifies with evolution. Again, it should be said that basic Christian truth will remain intact, only its expressions will change. But expressions are language and it is factual that language constantly changes. We need only remind ourselves of the great changes and additions that have taken place within the English language not only in history but within this decade of our own experience.

The logical conclusion is that changing the language does not destroy one's faith, rather it enriches the activity of faith in its search to understand the mysteries of God. When confronted with the challenge of speaking of God, man does his best . . . he speaks in terms that are meaningful and adequate for his time and culture. When the culture changes, language changes. Consequently, definitive statements of faith may be adequate for the generations of the time, but not adequate for subsequent generations. For Christianity to survive, it must be sensitive to the meaning of mystery and the difficulty in communicating mystery to ever new generations of men. God is mystery, Jesus Christ is mystery, coreless mysteries that must constantly be unpeeled as the future becomes the past. Mystery and future both demand that expressed truths always be open ended. This is the challenge that faces Christian thinkers today.

QUESTIONS FOR DISCUSSION

1. Why is faith more a search than an acquisition?

2. What is necessary for Christianity to remain a credible expression of belief?

3. What part does language play in the communication of mystery?

4. How does the Bible reflect the culture of primitive societies?

5. Why is religious mystery inadequately expressed in human language?

6. Can human language ever definitively express a mystery of faith?

BIBLIOGRAPHICAL REFERENCES

CHAPTER ONE: THE CHALLENGE

1. Van Buren, Paul M., *The Secular Meaning of the Gospel.* New York: Macmillan, 1966, pp. 63-74.

2. Altizer, J. A., *Toward a New Christianity.* New York: Harcourt, Bruce & World Inc., 1967, p. 83.

3. Moran, Gabriel, *Theology of Revelation.* New York: Herder and Herder, 1966, p. 20.

4. Schillebeeckx, Edward, *God the Future of Man.* New York: Sheed & Ward, 1968, pp. 5-17.

5. Bultmann, Rudolf, *Kerygma and Myth.* New York: Harper & Row, 1966, p. 3.

6. Robinson, John A. T., *Honest to God.* Philadelphia: The Westminster Press, 1963, p. 27.

7. Dewart, Leslie, *The Future of Belief.* New York: Herder and Herder, 1966, p. 17.

8. Robinson, *op. cit.,* p. 27.

9. Francoeur, Robert T., *Perspectives in Evolution.* Baltimore: Helicon 1965, pp. 34-36.

10. *Evolution After Darwin.* ed. Sol Tax, Chicago: University of Chicago Press, 1960, III., p. 107.

11. Teilhard de Chardin, Pierre, *The Phenomenon of Man.* New York: Harper Torchbooks, 1961, p. 218.

12. Robinson, *op. cit.,* p. 32.

17

2. Myth and Revelation

the meaning of myth · the social, political and cultural inputs of language · the origin of myth · man sacralizes space and time · the meaning of revelation · man's interpretation of God's presence

THE MEANING OF MYTH

To use a word in a way that is contrary to popular understanding is to risk being misunderstood. Yet, in discussing religious belief, the word "myth" is appropriate. Myth has a technical meaning in contemporary theological writings. It does not imply fantasy or fabrication. Throughout this book we use the word myth in the theological sense, the human expression of man's religious experience. What man speaks or writes about God is man's interpretation of the activity of God in man's world. These interpretations assume the color of human language. Myth can be erroneous but nonetheless it remains man's expression of his faith.

Myth is man's attempt to explain something he perceives as real and having meaning for his life. It can be a proclamation like the book of *Genesis* or the ancient *Enuma Elish* of Babylonia concerning the origin of things. Myth is man's explanation of his awareness of

18

superior forces and powers outside himself. It is man's self-explanation concerning the mysteries of creation, life, birth, death, and the hope for an afterlife. Myth is man's recognition of elusive powers over which he has no control. Myth is the expression of man's convictions concerning the origin and purpose of life which origin and purpose must be sought beyond the realm of the known and the tangible.[1] Myth is man's attempt to answer the very human question of *why* man. In the last analysis, myth in all its forms and varieties is the effort of man to express in concrete language his religious experience, his faith. When we speak of the Old Testament, of the New Testament, or an ecclesiastical proclamation as myth we are stating that whatever man writes or speaks about God can be written or spoken only in human language. This is the basis of communication. Human language, however, depends for its meaning and understanding upon the social, political, and cultural structures of the times in which the utterances take place.[2] Language is considerably limited and therefore, inadequate to capture once and for all the meaning of God or the meaning of man. The human search for meaning behind these mysteries is part and parcel of man's evolving history. The Old Testament and the New Testament are tremendous insights into these parallel mysteries, but they are historically limited and cannot be the final word.

THE ORIGIN OF MYTH

We cannot say for certain when religious self-reflection became a part of man's evolution. When man first came forth in the process of evolution, the struggle for survival in the midst of natural enemies would have been his chief preoccupation. When, however, man began to enjoy stability as a new species, his biological aggressiveness and instinctive desire for conquest then turned to horizons beyond his immediate surroundings. In other words, when the intense and initial struggle for survival began to ease, man began to reflect inwardly upon himself. The brutal struggle for survival was still very much a part of primitive man and still is, but deep within him there evolved the desire to understand. Self-reflection was born. And with the birth of self-reflection we have the birth of religious thought. The exact time of this phenomenon cannot really be determined. The first indications of man's religious thinking are found in the burial customs of the Neanderthal.[3] He was the first to bury his dead with provisions, thus showing belief in a world of spirits in the afterlife. Neanderthal, however, is not so very long ago. Some anthropologists speak about man's existence in terms of one million seven hundred thousand years.[4] Neanderthal goes back about one hundred forty thousand years. He is certainly closer to us than to his primordial ancestors. Cro-magnon man gave indication of religious ritual and belief by drawings found on the walls of his caves. The drawings are thought to be a hunt ritual and were executed in a remote corner of the cave, apparently set apart for the ritual.[5] Hunting was the chief means of survival of the Cro-Magnon. The origins of religious belief were often closely bound to the problems of economics.

Primitive man believed with conviction that his life was intimately related to the patterns of nature. His existence took on meaning to the extent that he understood himself in relation to the forces of nature.[6] The sun, the moon, the stars, the wind, the storm, the thunder and lightning . . . all these were powers over which he had no control. It was from the heights, from the heavens that primitive man sought to derive meaning. All the forces of nature seemed to rush out of the heavens. Quite obviously to primitive man, the heavens were the dwelling place of the gods.

THE ORIGIN OF THE TEMPLE

We know from our culture that the temple or the church is regarded as a sacred place. It is called the dwelling place of God, the house of God. This concept of a man-made building as the dwelling place of God has its roots in ancient symbolism. In the beginnings of man's religious thinking, the heavens were the dwelling place of the gods, of the spirits and powers. The sun, the moon, and the stars were themselves the mysterious bodies in the upper regions. The rain and the wind came out of the heavens. Lightning and thunder forced an upward and awesome gaze. His wonderment found solution in personifying the forces of nature as spirits of his ancient dead. Man saw earth as his dwelling place along with all the lesser animals. But something on the horizon broke the separation between the dwelling place of the gods and the dwelling place of man. The mountain rose up out of the earth and touched the heavens. The mountain touching the dwelling places of the gods became for man a sacred part of the earth. Primitive man venerated the mountain touching the heavens as sacred. It was the navel of creation, the place where the primordial act of creation took place.[7]

There were times when the gods were quiet. The sun went down. The moon was dark. The wind blew not. The storm was asleep. Where then did the gods rest? The mountain tops, of course. In the mind of man the mountain not only touched the dwelling place of the gods, but was their resting place. Man brought the gods to earth and in so doing sacralized his own dwelling place. Gradually, the mountain was thought to be the dwelling place of the gods as well as the heavens. But man began to multiply and spread out to the plains. The mountains became remote. Man, however, could duplicate symbolically the primordial mountain of creation by raising a stick, a totem pole, a temple, to represent the primordial mountain of creation. With these symbols man could sacralize any place he went.[8] Temples were replicas of the Holy Mountain and like the mountain became the dwelling place of the gods. Man could always find security and protection any new place he went, to the extent that he sacralized the place and made it the dwelling place of the gods. We find this concept of the Holy Mountain and the Temple to be as much a part of religious belief of the Old Testament as that of primitive man. The Hebrew God, Elohim, originated in the mountains of Haran from which Abraham fled at the time of the Hurrian Invasion. Abraham, however, took Elohim with him. Yahweh was the God of Mount Sinai, but Moses' concept of Yahweh outgrew the need for a mountain; not, however, the need for a temple.

When man moved out of the caves and into tents and houses, the tent and house became the replica of the

Holy Mountain, the dwelling place of the gods. The idea of the household gods is still witnessed today by holy water fonts placed by doors. In Christianity, the temple gave way to the many churches. Churches are sacred places, the dwelling place for God. Great church spires reach high, touching the heavens to plead the cause of man. The sacralizing of earth has a very long history and is still very much a part of Christianity.

THE SACRED TIME

Through the symbolic use of temple, man saw his place as the center of divine activity. Man's spatial existence took on meaning to the extent that man could continually recapture that primordial place of creation, the Holy Mountain. But, what about man's activity? Primitive man gave meaning to his actions by seeing his actions as repetitions of the actions of the gods. Man's waking and sleeping hours were repetitious of the rising and setting of the sun. His eating was repetitious of the great banquets of the gods. His own sexuality and the begetting of children mimicked the sexuality of the gods productive of all creation. Man's hunting the beast for survival was but a repetition of the primordial acts of the gods who slew primordial beasts hostile to the gods. All of man's actions became sacred actions to the extent that they were repetitions of the great acts of the gods.[9] To dramatize his cosmic relationship to the gods revealed in the patterns of nature, ritual feasts were initiated and multiplied. Through these ritual feasts primitive man could recapture the primordial acts of creation, birth, life, death, and even resurrection. An example of primitive ritual feasts is that of the New Year, a ritual feast in which primitive man could obliterate his guilt-ridden past by re-enacting the primordial act of creation. He began a new period of existence by restoring himself to the time of primordial creation. This ritual feast provided man with unending chances for renewal and escape from the boredom of routine or the guilt of the past.[10]

Through symbolic rituals, re-enactment of the primordial activity of the gods, man sacralized both his place and his time. To the extent that he sacralized the common he gave meaning to his existence. This was the dawn of religious experience and of primitive mythology. Primitive man's faith grew out of his convictions that the cosmos, the elements of nature, the great mountain, provided the key to his self-understanding. He felt intimately related to nature and her rhythms. From these rhythms, he shaped convictions which he expressed in the religious language of faith. Primitive mythologies are faith-expressions addressing themselves to the basic questions that confronted primitive man. These expressions were his primitive ontologies. They were also the beginnings of theology.[11]

Man's search for ultimate meaning, like the process of evolution itself, developed slowly and expressed itself in a variety of forms. We are not concerned here with the truth or falsity of primitive man's myths. We are concerned with the evolution of religious belief as man began to multiply and spread into new areas of the earth. We are concerned with the fact that no matter where man went he gave meaning to his life through the cosmological convictions he formed by his interpretation of the impact of nature upon his existence. The phenomenon of mythology is basic to man's growth and development. It was the basis for the expression of his self-understanding.

HEBREW MYTHOLOGY

Unlike primitive man, the faith-convictions of the Hebrew grew out of his sense of history. The Hebrew felt himself intimately related to the social and political events of his people. These social and political events were understood and interpreted as being pervaded by the divine presence. The faith-convictions of the Hebrew were more historical than cosmological. According to Hebrew belief, Yahweh-Elohim had chosen to enter the life of a small nation to make that nation his people. He would be their God and through them offer his self-communication to the rest of mankind. The success of Israel as a young nation and its ability to survive amid the social and political upheavals, lends credence to the Hebrew faith-conviction that Yahweh-Elohim was acting on their behalf.

There is a profound difference in the history of ancient Israel and that of ancient Egypt. Egypt experienced relative calm from the time of Abraham to the time of Jesus. Palestine was in a state of constant upheaval with the exception of small snatches of peace under David and Solomon. Israel was a small nation constantly caught in the middle of the shifting of the balance of power throughout the Middle East. One invasion after another walked the corridor of Palestine from north to south and west to east. Yet, in the midst of this international instability the small nation of Israel fought for survival and was successful until her destruction by the Romans at the time of the Bar Kochba rebellion (132-135 A.D.).[12] In this struggle for survival was grounded the faith of Israel and Old Testament history. The central figure of this drama was Yahweh-Elohim, the God of Israel. There was a human counterpart also in the figure of Moses.

With the Exodus and the Mosaic faith we have the starting point of Israel's history as a struggling nation. Out of these constant struggles Israel's faith is challenged. Yahweh-Elohim led her out of the land of Egypt with a mighty arm and an out-stretched hand. What he did for Israel during the Exodus he would do for her time and time again. Yahweh-Elohim would always be with Israel. During the Sinai experience Yahweh-Elohim was there, a pillar of fire by night, a cloud during the day. Yahweh-Elohim led them against the land of the Edomites and the Amorites. Yahweh delivered the land of Canaan into the hands of Israel, a gift sealing the covenant made at Mount Sinai "You will be my people, I will be your God." The rise to glory under David and Solomon strengthened the faith of Israel. Yahweh-Elohim had made them a great nation. Then came Solomon, the prototype of the infidelity of Israel. Yahweh-Elohim would visit his punishment upon his people. Israel's rise to power was a sign of Yahweh's presence and activity in their midst. Their decline from power after David and Solomon is equally interpreted as God's activity in their midst, leading them to repentance for their infidelity. The splintering of the kingdom into the North and South and the subsequent conquests and captivity by the Assyrians and the Babylonians were further signs of God's displeasure. From these sufferings would come the messianic hope, the theme of the messianic time when God would restore Israel to the glory that was hers under David and Solomon. From David the messianic hope took on the characteristics of a royal kingship. Under the captivities the messianic theme was expressed in the imagery of Yahweh's suffering servant. From the time of the Babylonian capitivity the Son of Man theme began to appear in Israel's literature (Daniel 7:13). The history of Israel century after century found its way into the Old Testament as a great drama and romance between Israel and their God, Yahweh-Elohim. The Old Testament took form as a theological history of the Hebrews. As an expression of their religious experience, it was mythology. The Hebrew religious experience had shifted from the cosmological to the historical. With the advent of Jesus, the grounding of man's faith-convictions would shift again.

THE CHRISTIAN MYTH

The Hebrews were very much aware of God's activity within their history. What Yahweh-Elohim had done for them long ago, he did for them in the present, and would do for them in the future. After the split of the Davidic kingdom into the North and the South, Israel, like a house divided, began to deteriorate, but the hope for restoration remained strong.

Following the return of Israel from the Babylonian captivity the work of rebuilding the nation began. But Israel would know no peace. The Persians who had liberated her from the Babylonians were overrun by the

Greeks. This initiated the long and bitter resistance of
Israel to hellenization, the enforcing of the Greek culture upon the conquered. It can be seriously questioned
whether Israel was totally successful in this resistance.
There is doubt as to whether the Hebrew writers of the
New Testament or the Jewish liberals of Gallilee were
really free from the influence of Greek thought. The
Greeks themselves were conquered by the Romans. But
this time the conquerors fell victim to the culture of the
conquered. The Romans carried on the process of hellenization. Israel returned from the Babylonian captivity with deep messianic hopes, which intensified as she
continued to fall beneath the foot of one invader after
another. Under the Romans, the Hebrew image of the
messiah grew into that of a great military leader, who
would drive out the Romans and restore Israel to the
days of David and Solomon.

Many Hebrew revolutionaries rose up against the
Romans only to be dealt with swiftly and brutally. Then
came Jesus of Nazareth. He was no insurrectionist in the
common sense of the word. He proclaimed a kingdom,
but it was the Kingdom of God. He preached repentance
because God's Kingdom had come to man's world. He
preached freedom not from the Romans, but from de-
humanizing laws. He idealized human sexuality in his
teachings concerning marriage and celibacy. He claimed
himself to be the unique agent of God's Kingdom. He
involved himself in the plight of the poor, associating
with social outcasts rather than the influential Scribes
and Pharisees. Within the Hebrew power structure Jesus
stood as a challenge to the stubborn law-makers who

bound the people to meaningless religious law and ritual.

The synoptic Gospels of the New Testament never refer to Jesus by the title of God.[13] Jesus did not claim to be the long awaited messiah. He did claim to be the unique son of God, son in the sense of prophet or king, not in the sense of divine. As God's unique agent, Jesus stood against the Jewish structure as a threat to the Jewish establishment. He placed himself above the human law of the Sabbath and attacked the Temple itself as a den of thieves. The elders looked upon Jesus as a political threat and with the help of the Romans, Jesus was added to the long list of crucified insurrectionists.

The freedom that Jesus preached lived on in the Resurrection. The followers of Jesus symbolized by the Pentecost, were afire with the new freedom preached by Jesus.[14] They began to proclaim this freedom, this salvation, this good news. And their proclamations touched the deepest desires of their hearers. Belief in Jesus as the unique agent of God's Kingdom and as the Son of God was the great religious experience of the first Christian community. Their religious experience and convictions concerning Jesus, shaped and reshaped the meaning of Jesus as the New Testament gradually evolved as a proclamation of witness to his life, death, and resurrection.[15] The believing community saw in Jesus the fulfillment of all the messianic themes of Royal Sonship, Suffering Servant and Son of Man. They proclaimed Jesus to be the Messiah and Son of God. Out of the living experience of faith, the Christians recognized Jesus as the messiah and Savior. These two roles found expression in the New Testament as a part of the mythological framework of the times. The Hebrew Apocalyptic Son of Man and Pre-existent Personified Wisdom were the context in which Jesus was presented to the Hebrews. The Babylonian Son of Man and Greek semidivine Anthropos were the linguistic frameworks in which the Jesus of faith was preached to the Gentiles.

We will in subsequent chapters deal more fully with these mythological frameworks in which the mystery of Jesus was presented. We are not concerning ourselves specifically with the question of the divinity of Jesus. At the time the New Testament was written there were ample mythological frameworks within Judaism and the Hellenized world to speak about Jesus in language and imagery easily understood and recognizable to Jew and Gentile alike. The first Christian community incorporated mythological frameworks not only in their preaching and catechisis but also in the language forms of the New Testament.

In the light of the mythological expressions used to convey the meaning of Jesus of Nazareth, we can speak of the New Testament as set in a framework of myths. This does not detract from the continually relevant kerygma. The basic kerygma remains. Jesus is the unique agent and son of God who proclaimed the Kingdom of God to be man's world. Man has the freedom and the responsibility of moving into the future. God's merciful forgiveness is always available to man's sinfulness. The forces of evil are a part of the human condition. Yet, faith in the agency of Jesus will help man overcome evil. The agency of Jesus operates within the community of man through the power of the Spirit and assists man in the job of building up and unifying the community of man. The community of man *is* God's Kingdom.

The Old and New Testaments are testimonies of faith by people who expressed their faith-convictions in all the rich imagery and the mythological frameworks of their culture. The writers did not write in a vacuum, but were inheritors of centuries of faith expressions. It is unrealistic on the part of Christians today to so absolutize the Old and New Testaments as to fail to realize that the biblical language was subject to the laws of social, political, and religious cultures. The Evangelists themselves were the first to rewrite the meaning of Jesus according to the needs of the community.[16] Once the Christian community recognizes that human language cannot capture definitively the mysteries of God, it will feel freer psychologically to seek contemporary expression of these mysteries. This is true of the Old Testament, the New Testament, the Councils of Nicea, Chalcedon, or Vatican II or any human pronouncement concerning religious experience. Faith is an ongoing process, part and parcel with the on-going process of human history. The faith statements of one generation of Christians should be open to further insight by subsequent generations. If a faith statement clothed in human language is said to be definitive, it becomes closed off from the experience of future generations. This seems to be the present condition of Christianity. New Testament propositions, statements by the Fathers, pronouncement by subsequent Councils, the utterances of Aquinas, Luther, or Zwingli, have been so absolutized by their respective followers that Christianity has become strait-jacketed in its own traditions. Perhaps, some answer to the present crisis might be found in reconsidering what we mean by revelation.

THE MEANING OF REVELATION

One of the most significant awakenings to come forth from the Second Vatican Council was the awareness that the very nature of revelation had become elusive because of preoccupation with the *content* of revelation.[17] For centuries, Christian theologians have been digging out of scripture and tradition this or that "revealed truth" or proclaiming with hostile energy the *fact* of God's revelation. Revelation deteriorated into a list of revealed truths. The scriptures were looked upon as the explicit utterances of God Himself. The truism of the influence of culture upon language, especially when applied to religious expressions, was lost. Much of what was spooned out to the generations of Christians as the revealed word of God falls into the categories of cultural prejudices.

Revelation is not the communication of a list of truths. It is the communication of a person. God created man. The ultimate answer to *why* He created man lies in what we understand to be God's will to share himself with another. Revelation is God's self-communication slowly and gradually to an advanced product of his creative act,—man. How God proceeds with this communication is a difficult question. Revelation is God's self-communication *to* man, but it does not rest with just the self-communication. It also includes man's response. Man's interpretation of God's communication is also a part of revelation. And how man expresses and interprets what he believes to be God's self-communication will be determined by the culture in which the believer lives. Man's faith utterance which he has called revealed truths are statements of faith clothed in human language expressing his religious convictions drawn from his experience. This is to say that, actively speaking, revelation is absolute in the sense that the absolute God communicates with man. Revelation, passively considered, can at best be the relative and timely interpretations of man concerning God's self-communication. The author of the book of *Genesis* was a believer writing at the time of David. He believed that Yahweh-Elohim was the creator of all things, in particular, man. He spoke of this creation in the cosmogeny and the imaginative language of his time.

The breakdown of creation into the seven days is filled with Semitic poetry. But later, man confused the poetry with the divine declarations of fact. We are not speaking here about the relativity of truth, as if what was once thought to be true was now false. We are speaking about the relativity of truth in that the language employed to communicate religious convictions was adequate for communications at that time. The people of that culture understood the basic kerygma in the terms in which it was expressed. However, these expressions are no longer adequate to communicate the kerygma. Our culture bears little resemblance to those of the Old Testament or the New Testament. This does not mean that we cannot benefit from the basic insights of these cultures, but exactly what these insights are is the challenge to biblical scholars today. By stripping these ancient religious insights of their mythological framework, we hope to avoid the error of confusing ancient truth with poetic imagery.

The Lord's Prayer serves as an example of culturally clothed expressions of truth. "Our Father who art in heaven" . . . implies the ancient separation of the heavens and the earth. This dichotomy of heaven and earth is repeated "your will be done on earth as it is in heaven." The Lord's Prayer in its original form used the cosmogeny of the day, a heaven up there, an earth below, a God up there, man below. Jesus in uttering this prayer and sharing it with others, necessarily addressed the Father in ways that his followers understood. But today, we no longer think in terms of heaven up there and earth down here. Nor are we any longer comfortable in the belief that God is in any way spatially removed from our own existence. It does not make much sense to pray in ancient language forms which do not communicate what we believe today. With no harm to our faith and with no disrespect for Jesus, the Lord's Prayer could be rewritten in more meaningful expressions, keeping intact the basic theme of man's dependence on God.

Conclusion

Revelation, then, is God's self-communication to man. This self-communication began when man became capable of self-reflection. God initiated His self-communication to primitive man through the elements of nature.

Man became aware of God's presence as his mind turned to the mysteries of the sun, the moon, the stars, the wind, the storm, the lightning and the thunder. These were the first vehicles of God's self-communication. Man was primitive. Man was young. God had eternity to bring man ever further along in the understanding of God's self-communication. Primitive man confused the vehicles with the reality they represented. But it was a beginning, a rich beginning in the history of God's relation to man and man's response to God. Man had first understood something of himself before he could understand the meaning of God. The history of man is, in a way, a history of man's self-understanding. God's revelation is also a history of man's self-understanding.

Primitive man came to understand himself and something of the *Other* in his relationship to the powerful forces of nature. But true to the general process of evolution, Hebrew man made the leap of self-understanding by discovering self-meaning in the social and political forces that operated in his world. Hebrew man saw in his history the activity of God. The dialogue of God and man seen through the eyes of the Israelites constitutes the theological history of the Old Testament. Like all written history, it is interpretative.

Another leap of man's faith took place in the person of Jesus Christ. Jesus was seen as the personal and unique agent of God's self-communication. Within the community of man there are those who recognize in Jesus His special agency of God's self-communication. But there are others who do not. And still there are those who do not believe in God at all. These are the faith questions and faith seeks understanding and expression. If those who are Christian wish to communicate with those who are not, they must speak in the language of men today and not in ancient tongues. And even after this is done, we can hope only that the non-Christian world will be sensitive to the expressions of our human search for meaning. This will also mean that the Christian must be sensitive to the search and the struggle of the non-Christian. Whether Christian or non-Christian, the future of man is our problem and our responsibility. Let each one bring what he can to build up the community of man.

Faith, like all areas of human existence, must give way to the forces of change of which it is an essential part. Faith utterances are myth, the human expressions of religious experience. Mythology is theology, an ongoing process of faith, seeking understanding and expression. This ongoing process of faith is an aspect of evolution, contiguous with the evolution of man himself. At no period of man's religious evolution can he call a halt and rest secure with any given "revelation." The fundamental error of Christianity is that it has led man to believe that he has captured in this or that testament or pronouncement the mystery that is God.

QUESTIONS FOR DISCUSSION

1. What is the basic meaning of myth?

2. Why are faith expressions limited to human language?

3. What relationship is there between primitive man's religious concepts and our own?

4. In what way can we refer to the Old Testament as Hebrew myth?

5. How is man's religious interpretation of God's presence a part of Revelation?

6. Should we rewrite the "Lord's Prayer" in more meaning-ful language?

BIBLIOGRAPHICAL REFERENCES

THE SECOND CHAPTER: MYTH AND REVELATION

1. Bultmann, Rudolph. *Kerygma and Myth.* New York: Harper and Row, 1966, pp. 10-11.

2. Maquarrie, John. *God-Talk.* New York: Harper and Row, 1967, pp. 55-75.

3. Noss, Hohn, B. *Man's Religions.* New York: Macmillan Company, 1963, p. 5.

4. Francoeur, Robert T. *Perspectives in Evolution.* Baltimore: Helicon, 1965, p. 116.

5. Noss, *op. cit.,* p. 7.

6. Eliade, Mircea. *Cosmos and History.* New York: Harper Torchbooks, 1954, p. III.

7. *Ibid.,* p. 16.

8. *Ibid.,* p. 17.

9. *Ibid.,* pp. 34-48.

10. *Ibid.,* pp. 51-92.

11. Maquarrie, *op. cit.,* p. 169.

12. Schurer, Emil. *A History of the Jewish People at the Time of Jesus.* New York: Schocken, 1963, pp. 299-304.

13. Brown, Raymond. *Jesus, God and Man.* Milwaukee: Bruce Publishing Co. 1967, p. 30.

14. Van Buren, Paul. *The Secular Meaning of the Gospel.* New York: Macmillan, 1966, p. 132.

15. Dodd, C. H., *The Parables of the Kingdom.* Glasgow: Fontana Books, 1961, p. 36.

16. Dodd, *op. cit.*

17. Moran, Gabriel. *The Theology of Revelation.* New York: Herder & Herder, 1966, p. 22.

3. The Creation of the Cosmos

the Babylonian creation myth · the Hebrew creation myth · the Christian creation myth · the symbolic language of creation myths · a contemporary creation myth · the first incarnation · the primitive psychism of matter

Origins remain an area of fascinating research for the questioning mind of man. No generation of man seems to have escaped the quest to know how matter began. Origins are not a question of *time*, but a question of *how*. Primitive man with his primitive myths was seeking to answer this question. For primitive man, all things had their origin grounded in the activity of the gods. The authors of the book of Genesis focused their answer on the creative act of Yahweh-Elohim. The ancient philosophers of Greece, Anaximander, Parmenides, Heraclitus, Plato and Aristotle constructed total world views to explain the problem of origins. Contemporary thinkers like Teilhard de Chardin also are interested in the question of origins. And in our more adventurous moments, we ourselves wonder about the origin of things.

Perhaps, this preoccupation with origins grows out of the conviction and the hope that origins hold the key to the ultimate direction human evolution will take. In the following pages we will address ourselves to the ancient myths of origins and offer a way in which contemporary man may express the fundamental Judaic-Christian belief that God created. The belief in God as Creator will remain although the descriptions explaining this belief may differ considerably from the traditional expressions. But then, this is what we mean by the evolution of religious belief . . . the freedom to develop religious thinking in terms of imagery that spring out of our contemporary experience.

PRIMITIVE CREATION MYTHS

One of the first recorded creation myths is found in the very old testaments of ancient Babylonia (Sumer). This myth of creation dates about four thousand years ago and was known to the authors of Genesis. The Hebrews were descendents from the ancient inhabitants of Mesopotamia (ancient Babylonia) and shared with these people the primitive myths or folklore of their ancestors. The *Enuma Elish,* "When Above," is the ancient Sumerian epic of creation.[1] It is a primitive myth expressing man's cosmological conviction that creation was the activity of the gods.

The great god and begetter of all the gods was Aspu. It was he who created the cosmogeny of the upper regions and the lower regions, the upper waters and the lower waters on which floats the mother-earth goddess, Tiamat. Tiamat brought forth all living things through sexual union with Aspu. Aspu, however, remained the great primordial god far removed from all that existed. Aspu begot Ea. Ea rose up against Aspu and slew him. Ea then begot Marduk who was destined to be the greatest of all the gods. Marduk was the sun-god. Marduk created the winds and the rivers. Tiamat was angry with Marduk for creating the rivers because the rivers rushing here and there disturbed Tiamat, the mother-earth goddess. Tiamat prepared for battle against Marduk and all the gods of the heavens, (We have here the familiar theme of the struggle between heaven and earth). A lesser earth goddess, Mother Hubur, an ally of Tiamat, created all the ferocious beasts of the earth to do battle against the gods.

The gods were not unaware of what was happening on earth. Marduk went before the assembly of the gods and sought the supremacy necessary to do battle with Tiamat. The gods gave Marduk the promise of supremacy. He stirred up the rivers he had created to disturb Tiamat and unleashed the winds to buffet her. With rage she retaliated against Marduk. The mother-earth goddess, however, was no match for the mighty sun-god. He split her in two. One half of Tiamat was placed in the heavens to become the constellations with their myriad of stars. From the blood and bones of the remaining half of Tiamat, Marduk, now the supreme god, created man.[2] This creation story of the *Enuma Elish* is a poetic and fluid human expression of the Sumerians showing their belief that creation came forth from the hands of the gods.

Theologically, what comes through in this ancient creation account is the primordial struggle between Marduk, god of heaven, and Tiamat, the mother-earth goddess. This expression of faith in Marduk, the sun-god, grew out of the experience of primitive man's witnessing the powers of the heavens attacking the earth. The wind, the rain, the sun, the storm, are the gods wreaking vengeance on the earth. The sun is the greatest of all heavenly bodies, Marduk, became their supreme god. Their faith-convictions initiated many rituals of worship and appeasement to obtain the protection of Marduk. When the forces of the heavens were benign under Marduk's leadership, rituals of thanksgiving were offered. When the forces were hostile, rituals of appeasement were offered. These rituals were primitive attempts on the part of man to deal with the many mysterious forces that surrounded him. They were also subtle attempts on the part of primitive man to manipulate the gods, and thus his own destiny.

THE JUDAIC-CHRISTIAN MYTHOLOGY

Barashith, "in the beginning," opens the first chapter of the book of Genesis. The first two chapters of Genesis are Hebrew myths that deal with the creation of the cosmos and the creation of man. It is, however, important to remember that the material eventually to be edited by Esdra (c. 400 B.C.) was written by a Hebrew believer two and a half centuries after the death of Moses (1250 B.C). Genesis was written, then, by someone totally committed to the Mosaic faith. These human expressions of faith were written by a Hebrew believer as expressions of his own and his peoples' religious experience. The authors of Genesis, as Hebrews, shared the creation folklore or myths of the ancient Mesopotamians. The task of the authors of Genesis was to put these ancient creation myths into theological terms understandable by a people long committed to the Yahwistic faith.

The Mosaic faith in Yahweh-Elohim gave a whole new dimension to the ancient Mesopotamian myths of creation. But this faith-expression of the creation myth in terms of Yahwistic theology, could not escape limited and faulty descriptions of the cosmos. Like the ancient Babylonians, the Hebrews believed the cosmos was divided into the upper and lower waters, with earth, like a huge island, floating on the surface of the lower waters. The rivers were caused by the lower waters seeping through cracks in the earth. A thin firmament divided the upper waters from the lower waters. This firmament was like a membrane stretched in an arch-like fashion from one end of the sky to the other. On this membrane hung the great luminaries, the sun, moon, and stars. There were several openings in the membrane which at times allowed the upper waters to pour through, causing the rain. Both the ancient Babylonians and the later Hebrews share this view of the cosmos. In the first chapter of Genesis, this cosmogeny is quite vivid, "Let there be a firmament in the middle of the water to form a division between the waters. . . . God made the firmament and it divided the water below from the water above. . . . Let the water beneath the sky be gathered into a single area, that the dry land may be visible. . . . Let there be lights in the firmament."

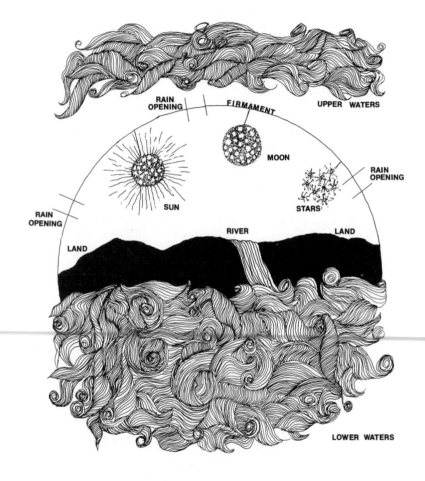

Figure I

The cosmogeny is unimportant except to serve as an example of how the Hebrew writer told of Yahweh-Elohim's creative activity. The cultural understanding of the cosmos pervades his writing. Yahweh-Elohim's spirit and breath swoops over the formless wastes. Then God, totally in command, utters a word and the word becomes the reality, "Let there be light." Light was the first thing to be created because of its importance. It separated the light from the darkness. In the *Enuma Elish*, it is the light or sun-god, Marduk, who became the supreme god. In the Hebrew account, fully aware of the more ancient *Enuma Elish*, the light (the sun-god, Marduk, by implication) is created by the mere command of the Hebrew Yahweh-Elohim.

The next three creations filled what had been created. The fourth creation brought forth the great luminaries hung on the firmament, one for day, one for night. The fifth creation was the filling of the lower waters with fish of every kind and filling the heavens with birds of every kind. . . . the sixth creation was the filling of the earth with living things, the last of whom was man, made in the image of God himself. In this first chapter of Genesis the author explained the creation of the cosmos by Yahweh-Elohim in a very poetic way. Hebrew parallelism runs throughout this first chapter. The creation of the first day parallels the creation of the fourth day. The creation of the second day parallels the creation of the fifth day. The creation of the third day parallels the creation of the sixth day. The word "day" does not refer to a unit of twenty-four hours, but serves to separate one period of creation from another.

When we recognize that the author of the first chapter of Genesis expressed himself in the style and im-

Figure II

DAY	SEPARATION	CREATION	FILLING	DAY
1	LIGHT FROM DARKNESS	LIGHT	SUN MOON STARS	4
2	UPPER WATER FROM LOWER WATER	FIRMAMENT	BIRDS & FISH	5
8	LAND FROM LOWER WATER	LAND	ANIMALS PLANTS MAN	6

Figure III   Parallelism of Creation Events

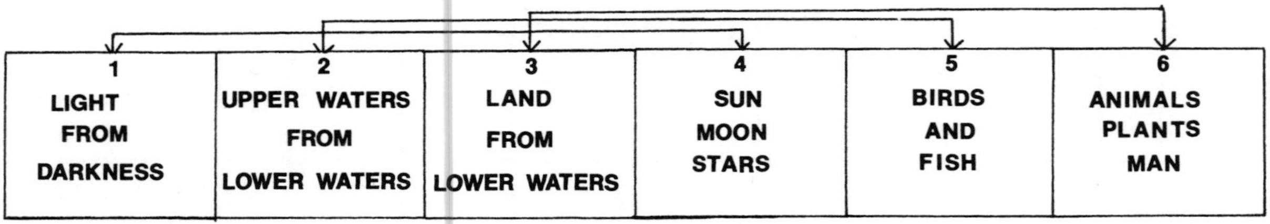

1	2	3	4	5	6
LIGHT FROM DARKNESS	UPPER WATERS FROM LOWER WATERS	LAND FROM LOWER WATERS	SUN MOON STARS	BIRDS AND FISH	ANIMALS PLANTS MAN

agery of his own time, we are less likely to confuse his symbolism with historical fact. What makes the Old Testament a difficult and complex book is our lack of understanding of the cultural influences which affected the expressions of the writers. The problem of language, particularly the symbolic language of religious expression, is a challenge to the contemporary biblical scholar and theologian.[3]

The author of the first chapter of Genesis using an ancient concept of the cosmos set out to portray the origins of things in the language framework of his times. His imaginative and creative writing was not an attempt to describe creation as it actually happened, but rather to speak theologically to his people that Israel's Yahweh-Elohim is the supreme creator and Lord of the cosmos. Like the earlier Babylonian account, Genesis expresses itself with a primitive world view. Like the *Enuma Elish,* Genesis expresses itself with a primitive world view. Like the *Enuma Elish,* Genesis attempts to explain the origin of things in the light of religious convictions. The authors of Genesis and the *Enuma Elish* use available faith frameworks. The author of the *Enuma Elish* explains creation in terms of his faith in Marduk, the great sun-god. The author of Genesis explains creation in the light of his Mosaic faith in Yahweh-Elohim. Both are mythologies because they are truly human expressions of religious convictions.

A Contemporary Myth of Creation

An evolution mythology as an explanation of the origin of the cosmos might be more understandable for the contemporary Christian believer. It is written from the viewpoint of one who believes in the existence and the creative activity of God. It draws upon the Christian belief that God ultimately is responsible for all that exists. It also draws upon science. With this synthesis of faith and science, the contemporary Christian should feel more comfortable with other new theologizings that are taking place within the community of Christian thinkers. The following explanation attempts only to be an insight, one among many, that may strike a meaningful note in the mind of the reader. Like all questions of faith-seeking-understanding, this explanation begins with the basic assumption that God exists and that he is the Creator.

In the beginning, the One whom we call God willed to share something of his existence with an Other. This Other would eventually, in the course of time, be capable of self-reflective response to the self-communication of God. But the processes, that would bring forth such a created particle of matter capable of self-reflection and response, would begin in a void of nothingness. This void of nothingness was the void of space filled with non-diversified and non-distinguishable sub-atomic particles of matter (or energy). This void of nothingness was the prime state of the Other which God created in the beginning. The Other was a space filled with sub-atomic particles that would gradually become more complex and diversified expressions of matter.

From the point of the view of the believer the cosmos is the result of the creative act of God. There is no contradiction to Christian faith to explain the origin of the world in terms of God creating matter fragmented into billions of sub-atomic particles, endowed with an exterior energy and an interior psychism or driving force.[4] This inner driving force would give matter the direction to unite and form ever more complex and physically intense expressions of matter.

The First Incarnation

God's creative act initiated the process of evolution. He endowed the sub-atomic particles with an inner driving force that would in time evolve to an intelligent "Other," capable of a loving response to God's self-communication. Not only did God initiate the Other but at the instant of creation he united himself intimately with the forces of matter so that in all the diverse expressions of matter that would evolve, God personally would be involved. We are not speaking pantheistically as if God and matter were the same or as if the divine energy and the inner driving force of matter were identical. We are speaking of an Incarnation: the assumption of the matter God created into a unity so intimate that he would for all time pervade all matter. The divine energy pervades the created energy. It gives direction to the inner driving force of matter. It is in this sense that I speak of creation as the First Incarnation. God, through the act of creation, joins himself to the "Other" of his creation so that in the process of time the Other would eventually be capable of a response to the divine presence pervading every molecule of being. The divine energy would thrust created matter ever forward in a linear line of evolution toward ultimate personal self-reflective unity with himself.

The First Incarnation is the unity of God with his created universe in which unity of matter processed through the build-up of ever more conscious and personal expressions. Matter, the "Other" created by God, would evolve to a state capable of a love relationship with Him who created it. Creation then is a primordial act of God initiating the gradual spiritualization of matter culminating in personal union. The First Incarnation is to be seen fully but analagously within the traditional context of the Incarnation of Jesus of Nazareth. The coming forth of Jesus as a human being hypostatically united to the Divine Father is a more personal and specific expression of the Incarnation of matter within the context of evolution. This Second Incarnation is more than the unity of God's creative energy with the energy of the cosmos. It is the unity of the person of God with the nature of man establishing a much more conscious, personal, and responsive relationship between the creator and the Other destined to a redemptive participation in the very eternal life and existence of God. God is not a power or a person in any way remote from the cosmos. He is very much a part of the cosmos as the all pervading Presence. Paul Tillich speaks of God as the ground of our being, the depth of our personalities.[5]

Within this framework, we cannot speak of God up there or out there, remote from or removed from matter. God became matter to bring it to personal unity with Himself just as we say God became man to bring man to unity with the Father.

The Swedish physicist Klein, calls these sub-atomic particles "matter and anti-matter" which in collision annihilated one another creating an explosive radial energy which caused particles of matter to unite and particles of anti-matter to unite forming universes and anti-universes, suns and anti-suns which today continue to move away from one another at ever increasing speeds.[6] Teilhard de Chardin speaks of these pristine particles of matter as having an inner driving force or consciousness.[7] This primitive psychic force of matter is responsible for the gradual uniting of the particles into the millions of suns of our cosmos. Our own sun is the product of the inner driving force of matter to unite and construct ever more complex and more intensely conscious structures. Our sun is a sphere of incandescent gas like all suns of the universe. And as is observable in all suns, an explosion took place within our sun causing surface particles to be thrown out into space. Removed from the immediacy and the intensity of the mother sun, the incandescent particles began to cool off. Still held within the gravity of the mother sun, the particles in cooling off began to form the various planets around our sun. Earth took shape as one of these planets. Swirling particles of matter developed the less complex inner molecular structures of metal (the barysphere), then the more complex structures of rock (the lithosphere), then the more complex structures of water (the hydrosphere). As the cooling off process continued more complex molecular structures came forth within the hydrosphere, and the building blocks of life, oxygen, hydrogen, nitrogen, and carbon took shape. The earth conceived the biosphere.[8] The latter is a fruition of the former within the process of evolution. The creation of the cosmos then is the initial incarnation of matter by God of

Figure IV.   The Evolution of the Cosmos

– the creation of the spacial void filled with primitive sub atomic particles

– the first incarnation in which God joins himself to the primitive particles in route to human intelligence

I.

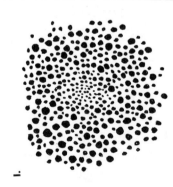

– our sun – condensed from a swarming mass of atomic particles – an incandescent gaseous exploding laboratory in route to life

II.

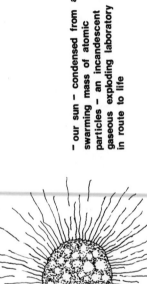

III.

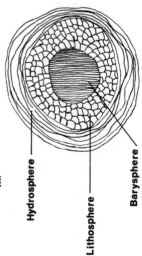

Hydrosphere

Lithosphere

Barysphere

– the condensation of molecular particles which during the cooling off period form the various layers of our earth–sphere

IV.

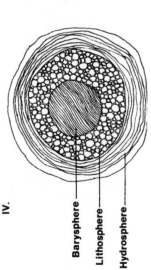

Barysphere

Lithosphere

Hydrosphere

– protein matter proliferates the hydrosphere
– under extreme pressure some protein molecules make the leap to the first living cells
– the reproduction of first living cells encircles the earth with a rich variety of living forms – the biosphere is born

which Jesus is a more complex and psychic expression in the course of time.

QUESTIONS FOR DISCUSSION

1. Is there any relationship between the Hebrew Genesis and the Babylonian *Enuma Elish*?

2. What are the indications of symbolic writing in the first chapter of Genesis?

3. Do we have the same right to express our faith in God's creation in our cultural forms as did the writer of Genesis?

4. Will the attempt to re-express our faith in our cultural language forms weaken our faith structure? Why or why not?

BIBLIOGRAPHICAL REFERENCES

CHAPTER THREE: THE CREATION OF THE COSMOS

1. Eliade, Mircea. *Cosmos and History.* New York: Harper Torchbooks, 1954, p. 27, 28.

2. Wright, Ernest, ed. *The Bible and the Ancient Near East.* London: Routledge and Kegan Paul, 1961, p. 270.

3. Schillebeeckx, Edward. *God and the Future of Man.* New York: Sheed and Ward, 1968, pp. 3-17.

4. Teilhard de Chardin, Pierre. *The Phenomenon of Man.* New York: Harper Torchbooks, 1959, pp. 56-57.

5. Robinson, John A. T. *Honest to God.* Philadelphia: The Westminister Press, 1963, p. 22.

6. Klein, Oskar, "Anti-Matter and Cosmology", *Scientific American,* 216 (April, 1967), 106-12.

7. Teilhard de Chardin, *op. cit.,* pp. 53-66.

8. *Ibid.,* p. 78.

4. The Creation of Man

To the scientist and the believer the question of man's origin remains a challenge. The latest findings of anthropologists date the origin of man at least to one million seven hundred thousand years ago.[1] The Genesis account of man's creation dates man about fourteen centuries before Abraham (1750 B.C.). There is no conflict between the scientific conjecture and the creative description of man's origin according to the Hebrew writer of Genesis who lived at the time of David or Solomon. From the framework of faith it does not matter when man was created or for that matter how, as long as God's creative act remains intact. The tension between a faith approach to man's origin and a scientific approach to man's origin arises either when science rejects the possibility of God's creative act or when faith begins to insist on symbolic descriptions as to the how, the when,

56

and the where. With the help of science, the believer can enrich his faith in the creative act of God. To ignore science in favor of symbolic descriptions of man's creation is to continue to widen the gap between Christianity and contemporary man. To transfer the symbolic descriptions of faith to definitions of reality is to open the whole question of faith to ridicule. Christianity has done this and as a result, it has become the rich soil of atheism.[2] The incredible things said by Christian writers concerning man and God has stripped each of its proper mystery and prepared the way for disbelief. And in our own time there are Christian leaders who still insist on ancient mythology to express the mysteries of God.[3]

THE ANCIENT BABYLONIAN MYTH OF MAN'S CREATION

In the final analysis the ancient creation myths of Babylonia, Assyria, Egypt, Israel and the Christian New Testament are basically the same concerning the creation of man . . . . man comes forth from the hands of the God(s). This is the message of each myth although couched in different mythological structures Again we encounter the problem of religious language. Like the Genesis creation hymn, the Ancient Babylonian (Sumerian) story concerning man's creation was first a religious ritual hymn. The Sumerians sang the hymn to facilitate childbirth. It was an incantation to insure safe delivery. It is common in history that ritual hymns find their way into Testaments. The Prologue of St. John, "In the beginning was the Word," is an example of a

Christian ritual hymn incorporated into the New Testament as part of the Gospel.[4]

The ritual hymn of the Ancient Babylonians sung to facilitate childbirth tells of the origin of man. Each childbirth was to the Babylonian a repetition of the primordial act of Marduk, their great sun-god. Christians, today, believe pretty much the same thing. They look upon the conception of a child as an immediate intervention on the part of God who infuses a human soul into the child at the time of conception. The Ancient Babylonian myth tells of Marduk and the slaying of Tiamat, the mother-earth goddess. From the flesh and blood of Tiamat, Marduk continues to create man, mixing flesh and blood with clay.

In the Babylonian account, there are two traditions. The one we have already given. The second account speaks of a mother goddess, Nintu, who mixes the clay of the earth with the flesh and blood of a slain god. Ea, the son of Aspu and father of Marduk, takes the mixed clay and places it within the womb of Nintu. Nintu then brings forth the first man.

In the Assyrian account of man's creation, Ea sings an incantation to Nintu, the mother-womb goddess. Nintu gathers fourteen pieces of clay. She places seven pieces in seven womb-goddesses, and seven other pieces in seven other womb-goddesses. The fourteen womb-goddesses bring forth seven male and seven female human beings. In all of these mythological expressions of man's creation, man comes forth from the hands of the gods. The origin of these various accounts as ritual hymns places the emphasis on the fact of man's origin in relation to the gods. The fact of creation is expressed in the mythological framework of the culture.

THE HEBREW MYTH OF CREATION

The book of Genesis has two accounts of man's creation. Chapter 1 to verse 4 of Chapter 2 belongs to the writings of the priestly source (6th century B.C.).[5] Chapter 2, beginning with verse 4, belongs to an entirely different tradition, the older Yahwist source (9th century B.C.). The first account simply states the fact of man's creation after the image and likeness of God. The second account describes the creation of man in a very warm and human way. God, like the great artistic potter, molds and shapes the clay in his hands and breathes life into the clay figure. The man is called Adam ("earthling or from the earth"). In this account we have the basic relation of man to the earth or clay as described in the Babylonian and Assyrian accounts. Both the Babylonian Lullu and the Hebrew Adam signify simply earthling or one drawn from the earth. Adam is a Hebrew word descriptive of man's origin. To transfer the imagery of the word 'adam' to the horizontal and historical plane of an actual historical individual is to miss completely the mythological form of ancient Hebrew. Christianity made the mistake of transferring symbolic writing to the level of objective historical fact. The basic message of the Hebrew accounts of man's creation (although the accounts differ considerably in their descriptions) is that man comes forth from the hand of Yahweh-Elohim, the Hebrew God, the Lord of all creation.

THE CHRISTIAN MYTH OF CREATION

The faith-convictions of Christians concerning the creation of man is not that far different from ancient Baby-

Ionia, Assyria, and Hebrew. Like the Hebrews, the
Christians believe that man has come forth from the
creative act of God. The Judaic-Christian God is, of
course, a far cry from Marduk of the Babylonians. The
question of how God created man presents more of a
problem among Christians than the fact of creation.
Some Christian groups insist that any explanation of
man's creation must include the idea of God's immediate creation or infusion of the human soul not only at
the time of first creation, but at the time of all subsequent conceptions of human beings. Pope Pius XII in
his encyclical, *Humani Generis,* permitted belief in the
evolution of the human body. But, he still insisted on
the belief in the immediate creation of man's soul, ". . .
for the Catholic faith obliges us to hold that souls are
immediately created by God."[6] It is difficult to understand how Pope Pius XII could say this when the dis-
tinction between body and soul is a philosophical conclusion grounded in the hylomorphic theory of Aristotle
rather than a theological revelation grounded in the
scriptures. The very language used by Christians today
to describe man is language loaded with the philosophical presuppositions of ancient thinkers. Philosophies
have never been considered "revealed" but some religious leaders in practice bind their members to primitive philosophical forms in the expressions of faith.[7] In
the expressions of faith which Pope Pius XII insisted
upon, philosophical language becomes definitive theological language. His scholastic assumptions did not al-
low him to express faith-convictions in ideas and concepts that grow out of philosophies more compatible
with contemporary man. We, however, insist on the

same freedom to express our religious beliefs in terms of modern philosophy as was accorded the Greek and Latin Fathers.

A CONTEMPORARY MYTH OF MAN'S ORIGIN

Much has happened within the community of man since *Humani Generis* (1950). Among Christian theologians, great efforts have been made to re-express the problem of the origin of man. The belief that man has in some way come forth from the hands of God remains intact. The problem concerning the "how" of creation differs considerably from the traditional point of view. The freedom for this divergence can be found in the fact that any philosophical explanation of man can at best be only one way of looking at the question. Any insistence on the part of religious leaders for this or that philosophical explanation opens that explanation to the criticism of rationalism. The language tools of biological evolution are equally valid if not more so than the language tools of Aristotelian metaphysics no matter how brilliantly they were applied to a Christian mystery.

To begin with, Genesis 2:7 is a human description of God's creative activity. God is pictured as having the hands of a potter and lungs filled with breath. With his lungs, he breathed life into man. This is not literal description as to "how" man was created. It is a poetic expression of man coming forth from the artistic hands of God. Science, on the other hand, has a few things to say about the "how." God is responsible for man's existence. To place this responsibility at the very beginning of creation rather than at some particular point in history does no injury to one's faith in God's creation. If anything, the conviction that God's creative activity initiated the on-going evolution of creation should enrich one's faith. Creation had a beginning, but it has no end.

The evolutionary process is one of the less complex and less conscious elements of matter evolving into more complexed and more intensely psychic expressions of matter. As we saw in the preceding chapter, the more simple molecular structures of metal began to form the inner core of the earth. As the barysphere solidified, the cooling off process continued and more complexed molecular structures began to form the sphere of rock around the sphere of metal. This layer of rock is called the lithosphere. As the layer of rock solidified, another sphere of more complexed molecular structure was forming, the sphere of water, the hydrosphere. With the development of the hydrosphere, there is present on our earth's surface the basic building blocks of life: hydrogen, oxygen, nitrogen, and carbon.

Within the hydrosphere the protein molecule was born. And within a group of protein molecules intense consciousness built up, seeking to make a leap to new and more complexed expressions of matter. At exactly the right moment in time, some protein molecules lept into the living form of bacteria. With the dawn of bacteria we have the dawn of life. With the dawn of life we have the biosphere. Life encircles the spherical earth. With the dramatic leap of protein to bacteria, the slow process of multiplication and union into ever more complexed forms of life began. As the bacteria became more complexed and intense, strange forms began to appear, called flagella. These had characteristics peculiar to both the plant and animal kingdoms. The flagella would themselves be the breaking off point for the two kingdoms of plant and animal.

Some flagella went the route of the animal called protozoa or the one celled animal. They multiplied by simple fission (dividing in half) and through the process of multiplying and uniting they formed the metozoa or multi-celled animals. Working throughout this process is the Teilhardian law of complexity-consciousness. The more complex an organism becomes, the more psychically it becomes.[8] The inner driving force seeks new ways of more complexed expressions. Some protozoa concentrated their psychic energy on the development of exterior skeletal structures and nervous systems. Others concentrated on the development of internal skeletal and nervous systems. The former are the arthropods, the kingdom of the insect. The latter are chordates. In this line there came forth the great ancestors of man . . . . the fish. Fish proliferated the waters Then a phenomenon took place The earth's inner spheres shifted and the earth's crest pushed up from its watery tomb. Land emerged as a challenge to the survival of the fish. The more imaginative fish ventured onto the land but they were ill-equipped for land survival. Gradually these initial land invasions proved less hazardous to fish who began to alter their structures to meet the challenge. Gradual alteration brought forth the amphibia. Some of the amphibia went the route of the reptile and bird kingdoms, while other strands prodded along more slowly. Some amphibia abandoned their egg laying habits in favor of internal womb systems. These were the mammals multiplying and diversifying as they spread across the continents. Some mammals concentrated their psychic energy in the development of swift limbs, giving rise to the great varieties of fleet four-footed animals. Others used their psychic energy in the build up of their nervous system and the center of interpretation, the brain. This process is called cerebralization. From this group would evolve the primates who gradually lifted themselves off their front paws, leaving their front paws free for much more dexterity and maneuverability. Within the diversified family of primates one group, in whom great intensity of consciousness built up, made the leap in the direction of man.[9] At the right time and under the right conditions, in a relatively small cradle area of Southeast Africa, man came forth. It was a slow and gradual process difficult to recover, but it is the conviction of anthropologists that man's origin lies buried with the non-traceable forms which constitute the intermediary species between that from which man came and what became man. Finally, consistent with the process of evolution and the law of complexity-consciousness, one group of primates, under the tensions of an intense build up of interior psychic force exploded onto a new level of existence. The centers of interpretation broke their psychological envelopes, leaping into the new envelope of primitive self-reflection. Intelligent life was born and with it a new sphere began to creep across the face of the earth, the sphere of thought. Man multiplied and filled the earth, with the dawn of thought, the noosphere was born.

Creation then is an ever on-going process. God's creative presence and consequently His creative activity pervaded every leap that happened within the process of evolution. There is no need to insist on an immediate or direct intervention by God in the creation of man if we look upon evolution as God's continual act of creation. There is no need to speak of God's infusion of a human soul either at the beginning of man or with the conception of a child now. Man results from the activity of natural forces pervaded by the existence of God! We are not speaking of God as some sort of world soul. We are seeking to remain faithful to the Judaic-Christian belief in the existence, presence, and activity of a personal God in man's world. This explanation goes the route of biological evolution rather than the primitive expressions of Genesis. Biological evolution can be substantiated by the accumulation of scientific data. All the evidence is not in, but what has been gathered points to evolution. The creative presence of God within this process of evolution cannot be substantiated by the accumulation of scientific data. It can be substantiated only in faith of men who share the conviction that there is a God. The fact that this faith cannot be scientifically substantiated serves better to point out the challenge to the mystery of God's presence in man's world.

The above explanation of the "creation" of man in the mythology of evolution remains faithful to the Judaic-Christian faith . . . man comes forth from the hands of God. The explanation of man's creation in terms of evolution does not lessen the challenge to man's faith that there is a God who willed that matter evolve to a level capable in time of a personal response to the creator responsible for its existence. The explanation of man's origin in the terms of evolution is demanded to-

Figure V. The Evolution of Man

I.

— every sun is a biological laboratory
— the potential of having planets within its orbit and creating on those planets the conditions for life

II.

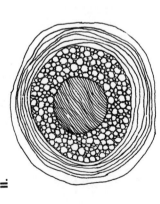

—our earth received from the sun its energy to produce life

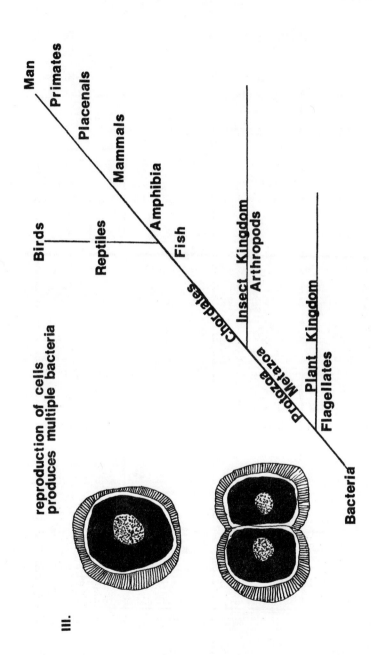

III.

day, not only by the data of biological evolution, but also by the evidence of biblical research. To ignore these demands is to court disaster in the Judaic-Christian education of younger generations.

It is true, however, that once we re-express the religious interpretation of man's creation we set forth a chain reaction. Religious doctrines are like a well-woven rug. When you begin to unwind one end, the whole rug is endangered. Once you begin to re-express the creation of man, it will follow of necessity that the question of Original Sin must also be re-expressed. A new approach to Original Sin in turn will demand a new approach to the redemptive meaning of Jesus. The belief in resurrection and the afterlife will also need re-expression. We are aware of the implications involved in the re-expressions of religious belief. It is a challenge, a challenge to faith. Our hope and conviction is that basic truths of Christianity can undergo re-expression while remaining faithful to the biblical traditions. The frustration is that the churches do not recognize their own process of history. Within that history, the biblical traditions were frequently recast in contemporary language frameworks. One great example is found in the hellenization of the New Testament under the Greek and Latin Fathers. Another example is Thomistic expressions of biblical faith in terms of Aristotelian metaphysics. Unfortunately, the meaningful insights of Thomas Aquinas deteriorated into the meaningless language forms of a Baltimore Catechism. The powerful and corrective insights of a Martin Luther fell victim to later interpretations that initiated centuries of biblical fundamentalism, insisting on the literal interpretation of the Bible regardless of the conclusive biblical research into language and cultural structures demanding nonliteral interpretation.

In the following chapters we will undertake the re-expression of some basic Christian belief with the hope of remaining faithful to the basic elements of biblical faith.

QUESTIONS FOR DISCUSSION

1. Why has Christianity become the rich soil of atheism?

2. Why is our belief today concerning the conception of a child similar to that of primitive myths?

3. Is the existence of the soul a philosophical or a religious question?

4. Why will the re-expression of man's creation demand a re-expression of our belief in Original Sin?

5. Once we re-express the doctrine of Original Sin what other doctrines of faith will require re-expression?

BIBLIOGRAPHICAL REFERENCES

CHAPTER FOUR: THE CREATION OF MAN

1. Francoeur, Robert T. *Perspectives in Evolution.* Baltimore: Helicon, 1965, p. 116.

2. Dewart, Leslie. *The Future of Belief.* New York: Herder and Herder, 1966, p. 53.

3. Paul VI, Pope. "The Creed of Pope Paul VI: Creation of Man", *l'Osservatore Romano* (English), 14: (April 3, 1969), pp. 53-55.

4. Schnackenburg, Rudolf. *The Gospel According to John.* New York: Herder and Herder, 1968, p. 223.

5. Anderson, Bernhard W. *Understanding the Old Testament.* Englewood, New Jersey: Prentice Hall, 1959, p. 384.

6. Pius XII, Pope. *Humani Generis.* Washington, D.C.: NCWC Publication 1950, pp. 16-17.

7. Teilhard de Chardin, Pierre. *The Phenomenon of Man.* New York: Harper Torchbooks, 1959, p. 78.

8. *Ibid.,* pp. 299-301.

9. *Ibid.,* pp. 157-160.

5. Original Sin and the Problem of Evil

primitive myths of original sin · the biblical basis for Original Sin · a new myth of original sin · human love and Jesus. · the meaning of Baptism · myths of the flood

The myth of original sin followed by the story of the Great Flood are included in one chapter because of the immediate relationship in most ancient literature between man's sinfulness and God's punishment. In the Hebrew Old Testament the Flood appears at a much later period than the narrative of the Fall of Man, but in view of the Mesopotamian roots of the Flood account in Genesis, we will treat the Flood story in the context of the Original Sin story.

Unfortunately, the Original Sin myth of Ancient Babylonia is not extant. About thirty-seven lines that deal with the fall of man are not readable because of the fragmentary condition of the ancient Babylonian tablets. However, consistent with other Middle-Eastern sources, we can reconstruct in general terms the Babylonian Fall. Judging from other ancient sources, the gods plan to destroy man because of his rebellious nature. It would be consistent with Egyptian and Old Testament writings to see the Flood story climax a build up of man's rebellion against the gods.

The Egyptian myth of Original Sin is not much more explicit. The myth dates to about the fourteenth to the twelfth century B.C. The Egyptian myth concerning the nature of man's fall was written before the time of Moses. Basically the Egyptian myth concerns the god, *Re,* who discovers that man has plotted something against him. *Re* calls a council of the gods and they decide to destroy man. A goddess is sent by *Re* to carry out the destruction. However, *Re* has second thoughts. He concocts an ingenious plan to save man. He gets the goddess drunk so that she cannot see man. In the light of this, *Re,* the Egyptian sun-god, became, in the eyes of man, a great savior.

Both the Egyptian and Babylonian accounts of man's sin, although not explicitly described, as in the Hebrew account, speak of the planned destruction of man. The Egyptian and Babylonian accounts deal with man's sinfulness in general. Both ground this sinfulness in man's rebellious nature. Man's destruction is planned by the gods as a punishment for his sinfulness. The Hebrew Old Testament is much more poetic and imaginative in the description of man's sinfulness.[1] The Flood story comes long after the Original Sin story, but it is a climactic punishment for the increasing sinfulness of man in general.

The Original Sin myth of the Old Testament is placed shortly after the myth of man's creation. The Hebrew author of the Original Sin myth (Genesis 3) lived some two hundred and fifty years after the time of Moses. The significance of this statement is that the Hebrew writer of the Original Sin myth is a man well steeped in the traditions of the Mosaic faith and law. He, as a distant descendant of the Exodus experience, believes in God's goodness. He is also aware of man's evil ways and man's infidelity to Yahweh-Elohim. He knows the suffering of his people, Israel. His fellow men are sinful men. They steal. They kill. They commit adultery. Their faithlessness violates the Sinai covenant between Israel and Yahweh-Elohim. The Hebrew writer is a witness to all the human misery poured into the life of any individual. Even his own wife or mother cannot bring a new life into the world without cries of pain. The hope of the Hebrew writer is that someday Yahweh-Elohim will deliver his people from all suffering as he once delivered them from the suffering of Egypt.

The Hebrew writer grappled with the mystery of suffering. Why is man's life so miserable? Why is life so filled with pain? His Mosaic hope gave him an image of a sinless-end-time, a time when men could know only the happiness of Yahweh-Elohim's friendship. The writer then projects this sinless-end-time back to the beginning. He explains the origin of evil in terms of a rebellion of man against Yahweh-Elohim shortly after the time of creation. The Garden of Eden and the Myth of the Fall are the creative and imaginative answers to the question, "Why is man so miserable?" It is an answer that tells more of the sinless-end-time of man rather than the beginning. Yet, man's suffering is explained by man's original rebellion against Yahweh-Elohim. The story of the original sin is the human language of the Hebrew believer who in his time attempts an answer to the problem of human suffering. Ultimately, his answer does not go much beyond that of the Babylonian or Egyptian answer. Human suffering is a divine punishment for man's rebellion. Yet, as a Hebrew, the punishment for the Original Sin is not without its hope. In due time Yahweh-Elohim will restore man to the primordial time of sinlessness. The Garden of Eden, the apple, the snake, the tree of life, the tree of knowledge of good and evil, form the mythological framework in which the Hebrew writer clothed his answer to the problem of evil. The tragic mistake on the part of later religious thinkers was to transfer these descriptive symbols or myths to the level of actual historical fact.

Most Christians today still believe that man's sinfulness began with the original sin of Adam and Eve. The confusion between the fundamental truths and the mythological expressions of the truth continue to hang up Christian believers.[2] We have already seen something of the creative and imaginative writings of the creation story. We cannot take literally the poetic expressions of the Hebrew author of the creation story. The same thing would be true of the original sin story. The name Adam is a generic term whose basic language root means earthling. Eve also is a prototype, signifying woman. The root meaning Eve is a third-feminine causitive-form implying she who gives or causes life. The word "isha" (woman) is also a generic term, the feminine noun form of "ish" (man).[3] To strip these words of their root meaning and to personify them as concrete historical individuals is to destroy the poetic simplicity of the

Hebrew writer. It also clouds over the simple teaching of the Hebrew writer that the misery of man is caused by man's unfaithfulness to Yahweh-Elohim. The question concerning man's miserable situation and the answer to that question are both expressed in the living situation of a tenth century (B.C.) believer in Yahweh-Elohim. However, his question and answer may not be our question or our answer today. The traditional understanding of the Christian teaching concerning Original Sin cannot be grounded in the Old Testament mythological narrative of Genesis 3. Contemporary biblical analysis and interpretation enlightened by an understanding of literary style, technique, and custom militates against raising symbolic language to the level of historical fact. Like the Egyptian account and the Babylonian account, the Hebrew Old Testament reminds us that man's sinfulness is responsible for man's misery.

The primary New Testament text for the doctrine of Original Sin is found in the 5th Chapter of St. Paul's letter to the Romans. Paul points out that through one man sin entered into the world, and through sin, death, grace entered into the world through the one man Christ (Rom 5:18). It is difficult to base the doctrine of Original Sin on this passage. The figure of the one man, Adam, played over against the one man, Christ, is not focusing on the historical fact of Original Sin as committed by Adam and redeemed by Christ. The interplay here is between sinful man, symbolized by the generic prototype, Adam, and grace-filled man symbolized by the generic prototype, Christ. Christ is the turning point between the period of alienation and the period of redemption.[4] This understanding of Christ as the central figure in God's graceful self-communication to man is consistent with basic Christian thought.

However, the traditional Christian doctrine of Original Sin, as the communication of Adam's first sin to all men, cannot be upheld by appeal to Genesis 3 or to St. Paul's letter to the Romans. In the light of this traditional misunderstanding of the use of myth in religious expression, a radical re-expression of Original Sin is needed. The same question, "Why is man so miserable?" remains a challenge to man today. The Old Testament Hebrew writer attempted an answer, an answer clothed in the understandable imagery of his time. His question and our questions are not the same. Too much has happened to the world of man between the time of David and the 20th century. The words of the question remain the same, but the meaning of the question differs. Death, suffering, the pains of childbirth, are not the wages of sin, but the wages of what man has not yet accomplished. Because the mystery of suffering for us is considerably different from the mystery of suffering for the ancient Hebrew, we are searching for a different answer than the one proposed in the traditional Christian doctrine of Original Sin.

A CONTEMPORARY MYTH OF ORIGINAL SIN

The dissatisfaction with the traditional expressions of belief concerning Original Sin comes not only from the results of modern biblical research, but also from the data of the physical sciences. A fundamental principle of biological evolution is meaningful here, for science would not attribute such a multiple and complex species as man to one set of parents.[5] In order for a species to survive it must come forth in number. The origin of man has its roots in many units that came forth in a relatively small cradle area of the earth . . . most likely Southeast Africa.

We are not rejecting the possibility that God could intervene in the order of nature to create man. We are, however, rejecting such an intervention as necessary. Such an explanation of the origin of man is not consistent with biblical or biological data. Stripped of its mythological framework, about all the Bible says is that man in some way comes forth from the hands of God. It does not tell how. Biological evolution tells us how man came forth, but it does not address itself to the problem of God. Yet, the expression that man comes forth from the hands of God within the process of biological evolution contradicts neither the limits of Scripture nor the limits of science, concerning the origin of man. However, the expression that man came forth within the process of evolution as many, does contradict the traditional Christian understanding of Original Sin. We must be swift to point out, however, that the fault lies not within the biblical expressions concerning the origin of evil, but rather in the literal interpretation of the biblical data by later Christians. How then can we remain faithful to the biblical data and re-express the mystery of evil or the problem of original sin?

In the chapter concerning the origin of man we described the origin of man in terms of process. Man comes forth as a leap from one level of material existence to another level. Man came forth from less complex and conscious forms of matter. The meaning of love as a power of uniting had to be learned by this new level of conscious existence. Primitive man carried over with him many instincts and drives of the animal world from which he came. Human love is of a different dimension than animal instinct. It is a dimension that is learned under the exercise of self-reflection.

In the first stages of human development, the power of self-reflective love had to be learned. Man came forth within the process of biological evolution with a basic inability to love. This is true of the child who is born into the community of man today. He must be taught to love. The baby has to learn not only to receive love, but to give love. The experience of the child born into man's world today is not so far different from the struggle of primitive man to overcome his inability to love. Learning to love is one of the key struggles of human existence. This is true of love of self, love of another, and love of the community of men.

The child is born then not only with a basic inability to love, but born into a community of men in which the struggle to overcome that inability to love is being fully waged. There is sufficient news-reporting to substantiate the tremendous inability of modern man to love. This basic human inability to love pervades the community of men on every level of human existence. It flares up between mother and father, child and parent, brother and sister, brother and brother, family and family, nation and nation. Original Sin can be described in terms of this inability to love, the struggle of the individual in learning to love, the struggle of mankind as a total organism desperately groping for the power of love. This state of anxiety, of groping, of multiple choices (many of which are disastrous) is the human condition of Original Sin. Original Sin then is grounded deeply within each and every human being as well as mankind as a whole. It is a way of describing the human situation that man has not yet learned to love. His nature is still very much a part of the lesser animal forms from which he came. Yet, his power of self-reflection reveals to him the need to search for love.

God is often described as love. The description fits in well with what we are trying to say. Man is in the process of unity with God who is love. Man is not God nor will he ever be God. Yet, within the best of the Judaic-Christian tradition, man is described as destined for unity with God. Our inability to love (Original Sin) is that part of our humanness that separates us from God. God created matter to evolve gradually to a level of existence capable of a self-reflective response of love to Himself. The process would be slow. The condition of mankind in general and each individual man in process toward unity with love is the condition of Original Sin. This is not to say that man has not learned some aspects of love. It is only to say that he is still within the process of learning to love. The proof as to the extent modern man has not progressed in this struggle toward love is witnessed in the burning of our cities today. Yet, compared to the human existence in the far distant past, cannot some favorable judgment upon man's progress in love be made?

What then of Jesus? If Original Sin is not a state of alienation from God caused by and inherited from Adam, what then is the redemptive role of Jesus? The question is a logical one. If you re-express in a radical form the concept of Original Sin, then the redemptive role of Jesus will also have to undergo radical re-expression. Original Sin is the basic inability of man to love. The redemptive role of Jesus is precisely grounded in his efforts to help man overcome this inability to love. Jesus is redemptive of mankind because he taught man something of the meaning of love. Jesus gave man a whole new thrust toward God in the struggle to love.

Jesus comes into the community of man as the unique agent of God's kingdom, of God's fatherhood. Jesus proclaims the presence of God's kingdom in man's world. He proclaims his sonship to the father, a sonship he willed to share with all men. Jesus, by his life, his involvement and his death, witnesses to God's power among men. Jesus brings hope to the people, a hope not only grounded on another level of existence in unity with God, but a hope grounded on the conviction that God's kingdom and man's world are the same reality. With the centrality of Christ within the evolution of human history, mankind took a giant step in the right direction toward overcoming his inability to love. Christ was a molecular particle, a spark of divine love breaking through the limitations of time within self-reflective matter. In this sense, man was redeemed by Jesus. He was given a vast insight into the meaning of love as objectified in the historical Jesus.

The child born into the world today is conditioned to evil both by his own basic inability to love and by the affirmation of evil by the community of man into which he is born. But, he is also conditioned to good. For, in the history of man, and especially in the light of the Christ-event, man has made some progress in his struggle to love. There are many signs of love within the human community. There is a growing sense of personal responsibility for building up the community of man. International organizations concerned with the problem of the world represent a breakthrough in man's struggle to love. As the child's life unfolds, he is caught between the forces of good and the forces of evil that are within the community. His own responsible decision will affirm the good or the evil. When a deliberate decision in favor of evil is made, the child rebels against God. By rebellion, he impedes the progress toward love which is God. In this turning away from the personal responsibility of constructively affirming the good of the community and adding to the evil within the community, the person senses his alienation. As man learns to love, he overcomes this alienation and confirms the power of Christ in man's world. The essential message of Jesus concerned the basic human power of love; love for self, love for other, love for God. And precisely in that order. Man is still an infant in this groping for the meaning of love. Christian man, now in the stage of crawling, has yet to plumb the depth of the redemptive insights of Jesus Christ. Man's history is long. His future is even longer. There is still time in the unfolding of humanity for Jesus to come into his own.

WHAT THEN OF BAPTISM?

With this understanding of Original Sin as that condition of good and evil into which every human being is born with the power to affirm either or both, what is the value of baptism? No longer can we use baptism as that

magical cleanser that gets baby whiter than snow. A
child is not born into the world in possession of the evil
forces. The child is not born in a state of alienation from
God. Baptism then cannot be looked upon as a ritual
driving out the devil from the infant nor an infusion of
the divine. Baptism does little or nothing for the child.
It finds its real meaning within the community. Through
the ritual of baptism, the community binds itself to the
child with the responsibility of teaching the child to
love. Baptism is the symbolic initiation of the child into
the Christian community, obligating that community to
concern and care for the growth of the child according
to its values and its convictions. This understanding of
baptism is a far cry from the traditional Christian understanding of baptism. The traditional ritual understanding is perhaps one of the most primitive rituals of
Christianity. The child is considered to be in the power
of the devil. He is in some way, through physical generation, stained by the original sin of Adam and Eve.
Baptism is that action that drives the evil powers out of
the child's soul. It pours the graces of God into the
child's soul and the child then becomes a child of God.
Some baptismal rituals read more like a horror story
rather than establishing sonship with God.[6]

It follows logically that in the re-expression of the
creation and the fall of man as attempted above, the re-
expression of baptism must also be considered. With the
Adam and Eve story and the myth of Original Sin totally
recast, the traditional approach to baptism cannot stand.
But in the re-expression of baptism, there is no desire
to reject baptism as a powerful and legitimate experience of the Christian community. The re-expression of

baptism offered above takes the focus off the child in the state of sin and alienation. Rather, the focus is on the responsibility of the Christian community toward the child. Baptism is a unilateral contract of the Christian community with the child whom Christians teach and assist in its struggle to love according to the attitudes and principles of Jesus as interpreted by the various churches.

THE MYTHOLOGY OF THE FLOOD

Because of the close relationship in ancient Babylonian, Egyptian, and Hebrew literature concerning man's sinfulness and God's punishment, we follow the original sin myth by the myth of the great cosmic flood. The importance of the Flood story in this chapter is not so much the sin-punishment relationship, but the great similarities in the Babylonian and Hebrew accounts of the flood. The Hebrew account did not borrow directly from the Babylonian account. Both the Hebrew and Babylonian accounts have a common source in the history of Mesopotamia. The similarities are too consistent to ignore the relationship.

The Babylonian myth of the flood is called the Epic of Gilgamesh. It is found in the eleventh tablet.[7] Most ancient people have stories of great cosmic floods. The Babylonians and the Hebrews are no exception. In the epic of Gilgamesh, the gods plan to destroy man. The remote cause for this planned destruction of man is man's general attitude of rebellion. However, the immediate cause of the planned destruction seems to be no more than a whim on the part of the gods. They want to end one era and begin a new one. The gods unleash the powers of nature against man. The winds and the rain beat upon the earth. So furious is the storm that the gods themselves become frightened and begin to cower like dogs. (Remember the account of the flood is written by a man.) One of the gods favored a man and instructed him to build a large ship. The man is instructed to take on board his family along with pairs of all animals upon the face of the earth. The man encloses himself, his family, and the animals within the ship. The rains continue and the earth is completely covered, even to the highest mountain top. When the rain ceases and the waters begin to subside, the man sends out birds to see if the land is dry. Gradually the ship comes to rest on a mountain top. The third bird released does not come back, which is a sign that he has found dry land upon which to rest. The man and his family disembark. Immediately, the man offers sacrifice to the gods in thanksgiving for his deliverance.

The Hebrew myth is quite similar. The names have changed and the context is clearly one of Yahweh-Elohim's punishment for the sinfulness of man. In the Babylonian account, the immediate cause of the destruction seems to be a mere whim of the gods. In the Hebrew account, nothing is left to whim. Yahweh-Elohim punishes man for his rebellious and perverse nature. Yahweh-Elohim is Lord of the cosmos and of history. His holiness and justice can no longer tolerate man's callous sinfulness. Yahweh-Elohim orders Noah, a remnant of righteousness, to build a large ark or ship. Noah does so unquestioningly, a sign of faith in Yahweh-Elohim. After the ark is built, the rain and wind lash out against man and earth. The deluge continues for forty days and forty nights (according to a priestly source of the flood story, the rains fall for one hundred and fifty days). When the rain ceases to fall, Noah sends out the birds, the first and second return, indicating that the land is not yet dry. The third bird does not return. The great ship comes to rest on top of a mountain. (There is a rumor that some biblical researchers have made occasional exploration trips in search of the ship.) Noah disembarks from the ark with his family and the paired animals. His first act is a sacrificial ritual, a covenant with Yahweh-Elohim. Noah begins a new era of mankind as Abraham and Moses and Jesus would do after him.

Similarities between the Epic of Gilgamesh and the Old Testament Flood:

1. The flood marks the end of one era and beginning of a new era.
2. The flood is planned by the god(s) and one man is warned.
3. The construction of a large ship for the man, his family, and paired animals is ordered.
4. The flood is caused by a cosmic rainstorm, destroying all life on earth except for those who are in the ship.
5. The vessel comes to the top of a mountain, a symbol of a holy place.
6. Birds are sent out successively three times.
7. Upon disembarking, the man offers a sacrifice to the god(s).

Profound differences:

1. Yahweh-Elohim is the supreme lord of all the cosmos and the history. Unlike the Babylonian gods, he is completely in control of the situation.
2. Yahweh-Elohim sends the flood as an immediate punishment for the sins of man. The Babylonian gods are rather whimsical in their planning.
3. The sacrifice of Noah to Yahweh-Elohim is a new covenant between man and Yahweh, a symbol of man's ultimate forgiveness for his sinfulness.

There are too many similarities between the Babylonian and Hebrew accounts of the flood story to ignore the interrelationship between the two. The Old Testament account is later than the Babylonian account. The Hebrew writer, sharing a common history with the Babylonian in Mesopotamia is aware of the legend of the great cosmic flood. He rewrites the story as a Mosaic believer, turning the flood story into a theology of man's sinfulness and Yahweh-Elohim's justice. Yet, Yahweh-Elohim is also merciful and makes a new covenant with man.

Both the Epic of Gilgamesh and the Old Testament Flood deal with the general theme of man's sinfulness and God(s)' punishment. The flood story unfolds within the mythological framework to deal with this general theme. Both are expressions of man's religious convictions. They are, however, symbolic expressions of man's situation and God's concern. Christianity has made a great mistake to transfer these symbolic expressions of interpretation of historical or cosmic events into detailed historical accounts of what actually happened. By pointing out the similarities of the two flood myths as well as their profound differences, we point out the danger of transferring symbolic and interpretative writing to the level of historical fact. We are not rejecting the idea that some time way back in the ancient history of Mesopotamia, a great flood happened. We are, however, rejecting the idea that either the Epic of Gilgamesh or the Old Testament account is anything other than a theologically oriented explanation at a much later date of what happened way back when. The Flood story serves as an example of complex mythmaking to drive home a fundamental belief that human misery is a sign to man indicative of the distance that remains between him and God.

QUESTIONS FOR DISCUSSION

1. Can the Christian idea of Original Sin be grounded in the Scriptures?

2. What is the problem with using St. Paul's Epistle to the Romans in relation to Original Sin?

3. In what way does biological evolution render the traditional expression of Original Sin unacceptable?

4. How can we talk about Original Sin in more meaningful ways?

5. If we express Original Sin in nontraditional ways, what can we say about Baptism?

BIBLIOGRAPHICAL REFERENCES

CHAPTER FIVE: ORIGINAL SIN AND THE PROBLEM OF EVIL

1. Hunt, Ignatius. *Understanding the Bible.* New York: Sheed and Ward, 1962, p. 63.

2. Schillebeeckx, Edward. *God the Future of Man.* New York: Sheed and Ward, 1968, pp. 10-13.

3. *Encyclopedia Dictionary of the Bible.* Louis Hartman, et. al., New York: McGraw Hill, 1963, p. 705.

4. Cerfaux, Lucien. *Christ in the Theology of St. Paul.* New York: Herder and Herder, 1959, pp. 320-321.

5. Teilhard de Chardin, Pierre. *The Phenomenon of Man.* New York: Harper Torchbooks, 1959, p. 185.

6. *Collectio Rituum.* ed., Walter Schmitz, Milwaukee: Bruce Pub. Co., 1964, pp. 11-15.

7. Anderson, Bernhard W. *Understanding the Old Testament.* Englewood: Prentice-Hall, 1957, p. 167.

6. The Call of Man

the call of Abraham · the call of Moses · the call of Jesus · the human knowledge of Jesus · growth of self-awareness · the prophets of today

Revelation has been described as God's self-communication to man. It also includes man's response. The record of man's response to God's presence in man's world has taken many forms in the literature of myth. This we have already seen in previous chapters. Our faith assumption is that God has turned the minds of men from the very beginning to a search for the mysterious Other. In the process of evolution in which matter leaped to a level of self-reflection, man began a search for God by a search of his own self-understanding. Man began to ask the basic questions: Who am I? What am I? From where did I come? For what purpose? What happens after death? In the attempt to answer these questions, man became aware of the great mysteries within him. The search for God began.

Some anthropologists have said that man's search for and belief in God is nothing other than a self-projection resulting from fear and anxiety concerning the struggles with life.[1] From the point of view of the believer this self-projection of man's basic insecurity in the face of a precarious life is precisely the type of human self-reflection that God envisioned to initiate the process of faith. Self-projection is an attempt to interpret reality. It is the evolution of this self-projection that leads to the evolution of man's images of God. Man in evolution is arriving at the ever new insights into the mystery of God.

Whether the search for God is man-initiated or God-initiated is a nonsense question. Neither conclusion is verifiable. Within the framework of the believer it is God who initiates man into a search for self-meaning. In this search for self-understanding the reality of God is discovered. God is the ground and depth of the evolution of self-reflection. And in this evolution communication between man and God evolves. From the very beginning of man there has been a mysterious dialogue between man's self-understanding and the discovery of God. This discovery has been recorded in many mythological forms, but at the depth of myth is man's attempt to express himself, to express his religious experience.

The question as to how man becomes aware of the presence of God in man's world is the other side of the question as to how God communicates Himself to man. The Hebrew Old Testament constantly portrays God's self-communication to man in the imagery of, "And God said to Moses." This is an interpretation not so much of God-talk, but of man-talk. The Old Testament as myth can, in the last anaylsis, be understood in the expression, "Man said that God said." This is not to exclude the activity of God within the Old Testament. It is, however, to insist that whatever is said about God in the Old Testament is said by Hebrew man. So much were the Hebrew writers within the Mosaic faith that whatever happened was interpreted as, "and God spoke to Moses." It is not difficult to put words into the mouth of God if one believes that God speaks through events. The Hebrew Old Testament is one long record of human words in the mouth of God. This is also a common practice among church leaders today. They give force to their human words by declaring them to be the divinely revealed word of God. This too is a question of faith interpretation.

It is a question of human interpretation because whatever communication there is between God and man must be by way of symbol. The question we are trying to answer is not so much whether revelation has taken place. The believer accepts this. The important question is *how*. It is important because it holds the key to the direction modern man can go in the future of religion, especially the future of Christianity. Scripture does not itself answer the question how revelation takes place. It simply interprets a series of happenings as God events and explains these God events as God's self-communication. But it can do this only in human language. In the faith of the interpreter the Mosaic interpretation of the Exodus is a series of, "And God said to Moses." Because of this interpretation that runs throughout the record of God's self-communication, we must be careful not to take the interpretation literally. Christians have historically taken the words of man in Scripture and objectified them as the words of God. Consequently, the words became frozen relics of communication rather than human symbols capturing in human words the presence of God in events.

Primitive man interpreted the happenings of nature as the communication of the gods. The *Enuma Elish* of the ancient Babylonians is a human interpretation of the creative acts of the gods. This is true of the Hebrew Old Testament also. The Old Testament is a human interpretation of the creative act of Yahweh-Elohim. Judaic-Christian tradition is the inheritor of that interpretation. With the shift from the elements of nature as the symbols of God's self-communication to the social and political events of a nation, revelation takes on more human dimensions.[2]

Faith in the God of history rather than faith in the gods of the cosmos is what separates the Hebrews from the Babylonians. Why God should choose the history of the Hebrews as the vehicle of His self-communication remains unanswerable. Yet, it is basic to the Judaic-Christian faith. However, there is no need to exclude God from the initial efforts of man to become aware of God. To arrive at a conviction that there are powers and forces beyond man over which he has no control is a major step toward the discovery of the ultimate Other. This was primitive man's initial contribution to the on-going process of God's self-communication. The sophistication on the part of the Hebrews to discover God more in their history than in the cosmos was a long process of self-discovery.

The Hebrews were believers in the gods of the cosmos before they were believers in the Lord of history.[3] This shift was not fully realized until after the Exodus, but it begins with Abraham. It should be remembered that the Abrahamic writings of Genesis were not written until some seven hundred years after the death of Abraham. What is written about Abraham comes from the faith of a Hebrew strongly entrenched in the faith of Israel after the time of David. Abraham is acknowledged as the Father of the Israelites, but the literary vehicles for conveying this fatherhood are myth. They are the religious expressions of a Mosaic believer.

The life of Abraham, therefore, is not a literal account but a poetic hero story, a constructed hero-biography. The author of the Abraham material lived at a time when Israel abounded in glory. The Israelites were numbered as the sands of the sea. The land of Caanan had become the land of Israel. All the enemies had been overcome, a result of the faith and covenant of Abraham with Yahweh-Elohim. What is written about Abraham is written in view of the historical accomplishments of Israel as a nation. It is not difficult to justify an accomplished fact by declaring God to be responsible. In this context, we begin the call of Abraham.

THE CALL OF ABRAHAM

At the time of Abraham there were great migrations of people. Ur of Chaldees was the original home of Abraham, a city located on the Euphrates River near the Persian Gulf. The people of Abraham were nomadic shepherds. They traveled easily in the desert areas of the Fertile Crescent. A great migration of people out of the Arabian desert swept northward toward Ur. The family of Abraham left the area of Ur to escape the invasion of the desert people. The nomads went northward as far as Haran, a city located in the far north of the Fertile Crescent.[4] Here, the nomads traded with the townspeople. They lived in their tents on the desert fringes of the town. Mobility remained an essential element in the economy of the nomadic shepherd. Abraham, like most desert men of his time, was a polytheist. He brought with him from Ur the household goods of the Akkadians. And as was the custom of the time, Abraham adopted the god of the Haranites. El Shaddai was the great mountain god of Haran.

While at Haran another great invasion took place. This time the mountain people from the north, the Hurrians, swept southward to the plains of the Fertile Crescent. Abraham and his family once again were compelled to flee. The motivating force for Abraham's leaving Haran was the invading forces of the Hurrians. However, during his stay at Haran, Abraham worshipped the god of the Haranites, El Shaddai, the god of the mountain. In facing the danger of the destructive Hurrians, Abraham placed his trust in El Shaddai, a faith and trust that would grow throughout the southwest journey to the land of Caanan. One major breakthrough on the part of Abraham was the belief that El Shaddai was not limited to any one mountain but could accompany him in his escape from the Hurrians. The subsequent success and prosperity of Abraham in the land of the Caananites confirmed his faith in El Shaddai. In the Elohist account of Abraham the El of El Shaddai is pluralized (Elohim) to indicate majesty and the Shaddai is dropped as gradually it was understood that Elohim need not be confined to a specific mountain.

When Abraham arrived in Canae (Palestine) he built an altar of sacrifice to offer thanksgiving to Elohim. At this time the commitment of Abraham to Elohim took the form of a covenant between Elohim and the people of Abraham. The fact that the people of Abraham had successfully migrated to Canaan, grew in number, and increased the wealth of their flocks, was later theologically interpreted by the Mosaic writer as the call of Abraham by Elohim, the Covenant between Elohim and Abraham, and the promise of the land of Caanan as a seal to the Covenant. The accomplished facts of Israel's history were by hindsight grounded in the Covenant between Abraham and Elohim. The Covenant itself is seen as a climax to the "call of Abraham."

The historical events of the Hurrian invasion, the migration of Abraham, his commitment to El Shaddai, the subsequent growth and prosperity of the people of Abraham are reconstructed and interpreted by the Hebrew writer in the literary epic of a chosen people. No argument is more convincing than success. In this context, Abraham became the heroic father of the Hebrew nation, and the subsequent hero stories of Isaac and Jacob are repetitive of the hero narrative of Abraham.

There is no deception on the part of the biblical writer in his imaginative and creative construction of the life of the patriarchs. The hero stories serve to point out the basic message of the writer that Abraham was a man of great faith and the father of the faithful Hebrews. The sacrifice of Isaac is an example of a powerful hero-story to illustrate Abraham as a man of great faith in Elohim. The basic truth concerning the Abrahamic epic is that Abraham came to understand that Elohim was a great God, greater than all the gods, and that Elohim was concerned and involved in the destiny of Abraham.

In focusing upon Elohim as the Lord, a deeply personal relationship between Elohim and the family of Abraham was initiated and would be repeated time and time again throughout the history of the Hebrews. Elohim or El Shaddai would evolve as the Hebrew Yahweh-Elohim, no longer a mountain god of Haran, but Lord of the cosmos and Lord of history. Abraham will always remain a significant figure in the Judaic-Christian tradition because his life symbolizes the breakthrough of God into human history. With Abraham, a new era dawns, God is understood to be deeply involved in the social and political events of human history. This breakthrough, however, is on the part of man's understanding rather than on the part of God's presence. He is always present.

THE CALL OF MOSES

By way of retrospect, Abraham was seen in the Old Testament as the father of the Hebrew nation and the father of the Hebrew faith. However, the nation of Israel owes its actual existence to Moses. He is far more significant than Abraham. It is Moses who, during the Exodus and the Sinai experience, shaped and molded the descendants of Abraham as well as many other desert people (Habiru) into the nation of Israel. There were many Semitic tribes enslaved by the Egyptians after the time of Joseph. The descendants of Abraham were one small group among many. Moses, a descendant of Abraham, welded these many tribes into a theocratic nation of believers in Yahweh. In the Exodus, the change of the name of Elohim to Yahweh represented the end of one era and the beginning of a new. The Sinai event established a New Covenant between God and the Nation of Israel.

Moses is the greatest of all Israel's heroes. As with Abraham, much of what is written about Moses should be understood as the feats of a great national hero. The sources for the Book of Exodus are not written until some two hundred and fifty years after the death of Moses. Again we are faced with the problem of stripping the Moses literature of its mythological embellishments. Even the *name* Moses remains problematic. It could be Hebrew or it could be Egyptian, but in either case, it is most likely a nickname for the great leader of the Exodus. Also, the infancy account of Moses is very similar to the infancy account of Sargon I, the ancient king of Akkad. Sargon, a poor boy, is drawn forth from a basket out of the water and cared for by a princess. He grows up to become the first king of a great nation. The infancy account of Moses, like that of Sargon, is a delightfully appealing story of the poor-boy-makes-good. Such an explanation of the infancy account of Moses does not detract from his greatness as an historical figure. There can be no doubt that Moses was a gifted leader, a perceptive and heroic man of faith. It would be just these qualities that rendered him useful as liaison officer between the Egyptian authorities and the enslaved Habiru (the wandering desert tribes).[5]

One day Moses witnessed the beating to death of a

Hebrew by an Egyptian overseer. In a fit of anger, Moses killed the Egyptian. The killing of an Egyptian by a Hebrew meant immediate execution. Moses fled from the land of Goshen, eastward through the marshes to the Sinai peninsula. The same route would be used by Moses in leading the Exodus from Egypt. In the desert regions near Mt. Sinai lived the desert tribe of the Kennites, descendants of Abraham through the line of one of his slave girls. The Kennites believed in the God of Abraham, but to them, he was known as Yahweh. Yahweh dwelt on top of Mt. Sinai. At the time of Moses a mountain was still venerated as a holy place, the dwelling place of a god. It would not be unusual for the Kennites to give their kinsman, Moses, refuge. He found a welcome home among the Kennites and married into the clan of Jethro. The life of a shepherd became quite pleasant. Both the children and the flocks of Moses multiplied.

But his people back in Egypt lived the drudgery of enslaved brick-makers for the temples of the false gods of Egypt. In the loneliness of the desert beneath Yahweh's mountain Moses felt guilt growing deep within him. His people suffered bitterly while he enjoyed the peace and joy of the nomadic shepherd. The dialogue between Moses and Yahweh had begun. The growing trust in Yahweh in turn gave Moses the courage to make a decision. He would return to Egypt and with Yahweh's help, lead his people out of the land of bondage. And so the drama of the Exodus began. Long after the death of Moses these few facts would become the Book of Exodus, a grand epic of Yahweh and his servant, Moses, in the struggle for freedom. The decision of Moses to return to

Egypt was retold in the religious story of Moses and Yahweh, and the burning bush. Fire was the universal symbol of the divine at the time the account was written. This symbolism is repeated in the description of the people of Israel traveling through the desert at night under a pillar of fire. In our explanation of the call of Moses there is no exclusion of the activity of God. We are describing the call in terms of the gracious movements of God within the sensitive and perceptive Moses. Under the psychological pressures of guilt feelings and a sense of alienation from his own people, and with his trust in Yahweh, Moses made the decision to return to Egypt. Prophets are born of such material.

The call of Moses, like the call of Abraham, is a response of a man to a situation that demands decision; a decision of faith and a decision of involvement. Man responds to historical situations with convictions born of sensitivity, perception, suffering, and faith, not by voices out of burning bushes. Moses' faith in Yahweh gave him the courage to make the decision to undertake the Exodus. With this decision, a whole new era of God's self-communication with man would unfold. The decision of Moses in the eyes of the Judaic-Christian, serves as a prototype to the decision of Jesus Christ, a decision not unlike that of Moses in the beginning of a new Exodus.

THE CALL OF JESUS

One of the developments within Christian theology today is a return to the humanness of Jesus. For centuries much emphasis had been placed on the divinity of Jesus.

The emphasis on the divinity to the neglect of the humanity created some unhealthy effects within Christianity. Jesus was pushed more and more into the sphere of the divine. Christians began to look around for another intermediary between the divine and the human. Mary, the mother of Jesus, seemed to fill this need. It was not so long ago when Marian novenas were attended with as much, if not more, devotion and enthusiasm than was the celebration of the Eucharist.

The reemphasis upon the humanness of Jesus is not without its problems. In some theological circles a questioning of the divinity of Jesus has developed. This question has begun to cut across most denominations of Christians. Perhaps this is due to the swing of the pendulum from the over-emphasis on the divinity of Jesus to the over-emphasis on the humanity of Jesus. There could be, however, a deeper question. Is the word "divine" the best human symbol to describe the relationship of Jesus to God? Even to use the word "Son" in terms of Jesus as Divine Son of God is to make a human construction of relationship, son to father, to explain the relationship of Jesus to Yahweh. In a later chapter the problem of Jesus will be discussed. Our present concern centers on the call of Jesus as a man responding to a human situation, a call similar to that of Abraham and Moses.

The call of Jesus to do the work of the father involves the consciousness of Jesus. Traditionally, we have understood Jesus to be true God and true man. Traditionally, Jesus was the union of the divine and the human. Jesus was both God and Man. These language constructs attempt to describe the relationship of Jesus to God.

Yet, no matter what the language, the relationship of Jesus to God will remain the essential Christian mystery. And mystery implies our inability to express the reality adequately either in concept or word. In the last analysis, Jesus reveals the relationship of divine consciousness with human consciousness.

The human consciousness of Jesus was fully human. There is no biblical evidence that Jesus had an omniscient human consciousness endowed with beatific vision.[6] Some Christian traditions would have us believe that at the very instant of conception Jesus was omniscient.[7] Such an idea cannot be grounded in the Scriptures. It can be grounded in the later Greek concepts concerning knowledge as the highest perfection of human existence. It was not a big step to endow the Son of God's human nature with the most perfect knowledge possible.

Knowledge of beatific vision is that knowledge said to be enjoyed only by those who are in God's presence in heaven. Not only is the notion of beatific vision as a part of the consciousness of Jesus nonbiblical, it is destructive of the human consciousness of Jesus. It is not within the human experience of consciousness to be omniscient at the time of conception or during one's infancy. The human consciousness of Jesus grew according to the laws of human growth. Whatever communication God would make to the human consciousness of Jesus would be according to the true humanness of consciousness. Jesus was not aware of any relationship to the divine until that consciousness became self-reflective. Even then, the self-awareness of Jesus would be a gradual development. This does not deny the relationship of unity between Jesus and God from the moment of conception. However, awareness of this unity could not be possible until the consciousness of Jesus reached a certain point in his development. Through inner moments of self-awareness Jesus began to understand vaguely, intuitively, and in an undefined way, the total reality that was Himself.[8]

A man is self-conscious of his person. Yet, only through long experience does a man understand himself. Every human being has a spiritual history, a history of inner growth within the social structures of interpersonal relations and conflicts into which he is born. A man comes to an understanding of himself in terms of his inner self-image constructed out of the raw material of living experience. Such a progressive (or retrogressive) self-interpretation becomes clarified and articulated through the challenges of love and conflict. It is these that reveal a man to himself. We begin to know ourselves in light of our reactions to persons, situations, and things.

This description of human consciousness describes the development of Jesus' self-awareness of His relationship to the divine. This self-awareness would grow, increase and become articulate through His struggles and confrontations with the Jewish community, His family life, His public life, His political involvement, His faith in Yahweh, His rejection by the people, the love of His disciples, His sufferings, these gradually revealed to Him His mission and His relation to God.

The call of Jesus, like the call of Abraham and Moses, was a human response of His human consciousness to God in the face of a situation that required a decision. Jesus believed in the Hebrew conviction that God acted in man's world.[9] He was also convinced that God's kingdom and man's were the same. He understood His mission to be one of proclaiming the kingdom of God to be here and now, present in man's world. This understanding would be a gradual development. At first Jesus was a follower of the movement of John the Baptizer. Jesus himself, through baptism, was initiated into the followers of John. Gradually, Jesus parted company with John because John was a separatist, a monastic far removed from the needs of the people. It was to the cities and not to the desert that Jesus felt the kingdom of God should be preached. Jesus would take his message to the people, the poor, the blind, the oppressed, and the ignorant.

The Jewish leaders had little concern for the common people. They burdened them with meaningless laws and its consequent anxiety. Jesus sought to liberate them from these laws and anxieties by preaching the freedom of love and the forgiveness of God. He flaunted the Sabbath. Man was more important than the law of the Sabbath, (Matt. 12:1-14) Jesus rebelled against the oppressive legalistic religious laws. Yahweh, the God of human concern, had deteriorated into a God of law, a judge. Jesus preached Yahweh as the divine forgiver, a patient and loving Lord.

Jesus' struggle to free the people from the superstition of the law became an intense conflict with the establishment. In this conflict Jesus understood more and more his unique relationship to Yahweh. He understood himself to be the son of God, a sonship he offered to share with His fellow men. As the opposition to His mission grew, the depth of his faith in the Father intensified.

He came to understand himself as the unique agent of God's kingdom and He preached God's kingdom to all who would listen. The call of Jesus was the response of Jesus to the needs of the people, the response to preach the hopefulness of God's kingdom, a kingdom not to be waited for, but one to be built up within the living community of men. For this radical departure from the established religion and social structure, Jesus paid with His life.

Conclusion

The decisions and the subsequent actions of Abraham, Moses, and Jesus grew out of their faith-convictions. In the struggle of their actions, their faith-convictions intensified. They were exceptional men who took hold of a human situation with all their energy and poured themselves out, according to their self-understanding of God. Each one, because of his faith-convictions, initiated new eras of religious experience. The human situation that called them to a faith response is still very much a part of the human community. The threat of war and devastation hangs over the world of men like the sword of Damocles. Oppression of the poor has turned the world into one large revolution of the southern hemisphere against the northern hemisphere. The superstitious burden of religious law and the religious ethic built into civil law continues to alienate the youth of our society. There is as much a need for the prophets to come forth today and proclaim the presence of God in man's world as there was at the time of Jesus.

The call comes to men today in the same way it came to Abraham, Moses, and Jesus—through the human situation, through the social, political, and the religious structures of our world. The call to man is always there. The response is there, also. The lives of many men are poured out in the building of the community of man. But, we are a dull generation. We would rather turn to the words of Moses and Jesus in their historical situations than listen to the prophets of our own time.

And who are these prophets? The answer to this question is just as difficult as it was for the Jews confronted by Jesus. Perhaps, like our counterparts of long ago, we kill our prophets or cast them *inside* the walls. Few whites would call Martin Luther King a prophet, yet he responded to a call, a dream. Few would call Malcolm X a prophet, yet he responded to a call on behalf of his people.

The question of who is a prophet will always involve ambiguity. The Hebrews and the Romans at the time of Jesus failed to recognize a prophet. It is not our concern here to say who is a prophet and who is not. The concern is that prophets are among us. And the concern is that we are so past-oriented to the prophets of old that we miss the prophets of today. The call of God to men to respond to the human condition is itself a part of the human situation. The response of men to that call is also a part of our human condition. The obligation of followers of prophets is to listen to their words.

QUESTIONS FOR DISCUSSION

1. Why is Moses more significant than Abraham in the Judaic-Christian tradition?

2. How were the Kennites related to Moses?

3. In the call of Moses was the burning bush a poetic symbol or an historical fact?

4. Was the human consciousness of Jesus subject to the laws of human growth?

5. When did Jesus fully realize the nature of his relationship to God?

BIBLIOGRAPHICAL REFERENCES

Chapter Six: The Call of Man

1. Dewart, Leslie. *The Future of Belief.* New York: Herder and Herder, 1966, p. 21.

2. Eliade, Mircea. *Cosmos and History.* New York: Harper Torchbooks, 1959, p. 104.

3. Anderson, Bernhard W. *Understanding the Old Testament.* Englewood: Prentice-Hall, 1957, p. 23.

4. *Ibid.,* p. 16.

5. *Ibid.,* p. 31.

6. Brown, Raymond. *Jesus God and Man.* Milwaukee: The Bruce Pub. Co., 1967, pp. 39-102.

7. *The Church Teaches,* ed., John F. Clarkson et al., St. Louis: B. Herder Co., 1960, p. 197.

8. Moran, Gabriel. *Theology of Revelation.* New York: Herder and Herder, 1966, pp. 68-71.

9. Dodd, C. H. *The Parables of the Kingdom.* Glasgow: Fontana, 1961, p. 36.

7. The Relation of God to the Man Jesus: The Second Incarnation

the second incarnation · the ambiguity of the Synoptic Gospels · the Babylonian son of man · the Greek Anthropos · the hypostatic union

The World Council of Churches defined a Christian as one who believes in Jesus of Nazareth as the Divine Son of God.[1] Christians who believe in the divinity of Jesus are certainly in the majority. There is, however, a growing number of Christians who do not consider the question of the divinity of Jesus as relevant. Their concern, like that of the first Christian community, is more in the light of what Jesus did, not what he was. These Christians consider Jesus to be the greatest of God's prophets, the personal vehicle of God's self-communication to man concerning authentic human existence.

No matter what answer is given to the question concerning the divinity of Jesus, the underlying mystery will continue to challenge every generation of Christians, "What is the relationship of Jesus to God?"[2] Answers to this question constitute a great part of the history of Christianity. The New Testament community addressed itself to the question. John and Paul do not hesitate to give title of divinity to Jesus.[3] Yet, Matthew, Mark and Luke run shy of the title "divine" in reference to Jesus. The Synoptic Gospels consistent with the Hebrew tradition reserve the title of God for Yahweh. The New Testament is hesitant if not ambiguous in describing Jesus as divine. The human expressions of Paul and John to describe Jesus as divine were already a part of the language frameworks of Jews and Gentiles throughout the Middle East. The Hebrew Apocalyptic Son of Man and Personified Wisdom offer one framework in which to describe Jesus. The Babylonian Son of Man offers another framework in which to speak about Jesus. The writers did not begin in a vacuum. They wished to share their religious experience of Jesus. The only meaningful way in which to communicate to others their faith in Jesus would be in language structures recognizable by their hearers and readers. The content of this chapter will direct itself to the various myth frameworks available to the Christian writers at the time of the New Testament writing. There is no intention here of rejecting the divinity of Jesus. The focus is on the various ways available to the first Christians in which to speak of Jesus.

THE BABYLONIAN SON OF MAN

Long before the appearance of Jesus within the community of man, the Babylonians believed in the coming of the God-man. This ancient Son of Man myth was well known throughout the Middle East. The Greeks had incorporated it into their mythology under the title of the god, *Anthropos*. In Judaism at the time of the Babylonian Captivity the Son of Man theme became a part of the Hebrew literature of Daniel. Daniel had transformed it into a corporate symbol of the people of Israel. In later Judaism however, during the Maccabean period, there were strains of the Son of Man existing independent of the seventh chapter of Daniel. Outside of the conservative circles in Jerusalem, the Babylonian Son of Man and the Hebrew Messiah grew closer into one image.[4]

The Babylonian Son of Man myth had its roots in the more ancient myth of primordial man. Primordial man was not an Adam. Rather, he was a god-who-was-like-man. Primordial man was divine by nature, arrayed in all the glory of the gods. He was the son of the most high god. He dwelt on high with the Lord of the cosmos as one always existing. Yet, he was created by the great Lord so that he in turn would bring forth creation. He was king of paradise and prototype of all righteous men. He had as attributes wisdom and understanding, an eschatological figure who in the end of time would establish paradise for all men. He would be victorious over the forces of evil. Presently he was hidden within the most high god, but one day would come on the clouds in glory to judge the living and the dead. This is the Babylonian description of their god, the Son of Man.[5]

This Babylonian description of the Son of Man is not too far removed from the Christian description of Jesus of Nazareth placed in a monotheistic framework. Is there any relationship between the Christian idea of Incarnation and the Babylonian Son of Man myth? Before we answer this question we will take a look at the Greek god, *Anthropos* (the Greek word for Man). The Greek god, *Anthropos,* was a divine preexistent being who came into existence before all creation. He was in some way the prototype of all creation, the divine being closest to creation. He was a cosmic figure, the mystical expression of the world. He was the first man, the preacher of righteousness. He would redeem man from his material prison. He was created to liberate man from evil. He would be the redeemer and savior of all mankind and his spirit would dwell in those who would follow his ways. He would reveal himself to men by coming on the clouds in glory and he would bring resurrection to all men.[6]

The similarity between the Greek god, *Anthropos,* and the Babylonian Son of Man is too great to be overlooked. The continuity between the two can historically be traced from the Babylonian whom the Persians conquered to the Greeks who conquered the Persians. The basic Son of Man themes are found in Babylonian, Persian and Greek religious writings. Later, Greek Gnosticism, especially in terms of the Logos theme, is but a further expression of the Babylonian Son of Man.

In the development of the messianic theme in canonical Hebrew literature, the Son of Man myth never really took hold. The Hebrews were committed monotheists. They could not accept any concept of divinity other than Yahweh. Yahweh alone was the creator of the cosmos, the Lord of history and judge of mankind.

The Hebrew messiah and the Babylonian Son of Man have no literary interdependence. It is true that Daniel refers to the Son of Man, but only as a corporate symbol of Israel, not as a messianic individual. In general, the only hint of supernaturalism or divinity that creeps into the Hebrew messianic themes is found in the theme of Royal Kingship.[7] The messiah was to be of the royal line of David and as a king, he would be identified with the divine.

In Jewish literature of the Maccabean period, the Babylonian Son of Man began to make an appearance. The Ethiopian Book of Enoch spoke about the eschatological role of the Son of Man who would judge the world and rule all men of righteousness. Also in the Syrian Apocalypse of Baruch, the Babylonian Son of Man and the Hebrew Messiah are intermingled. Consequently, outside of the conservative circles of Jews who resisted any form of hellenization, other circles of Jews incorporated outside influences into their own religious thinking. One of the circles most susceptible to outside influences was the Galileans. They lived far removed from the orthodoxy of Jerusalem and were a minority among the Gentiles. Jesus and his immediate followers were Galileans. To what extent they were influenced by the Greek input of the god *Anthropos* and the intermingling of the Messiah and the Son of Man remains a difficult question. But that they were exposed to these frameworks of myths does not seem possible to deny. The question becomes even more significant when throughout the New Testament the very title Jesus (or his writers) used as self-identification was precisely that of the Son of Man. Jesus avoided the Hebrew title of Messiah in favor of the Gentile title Son of Man. Furthermore, in the writings of John, the logos theme of John's prologue conveys much of the preexistent notion of the Greek *Anthropos,* granting however, that the Greek influence was by way of the Wisdom Literature of the Old Testament.[8]

The focus we are suggesting is that the New Testament interpretation of the relationship of Jesus to Yahweh is described in the already existing myth frameworks of the Hebrew Apocalyptic preexistent Wisdom, the Greek Anthropos and the Babylonian Son of Man. The preaching of Jesus within these categories would have been understood by a vast number of people living throughout the hellenized world, with the exception of the conservative Jewish community which had remained faithful to the resistance against hellenization.

THE CHRISTIAN MYTH OF INCARNATION: The Hypostatic Union

The growth of Christianity within the Jewish community inevitably led to tension. Outbreaks of hostility were periodic. The final break between the Jews and the Christians took place at the time of the Bar Cochba rebellion (132 A.D.). Bar Cochba proclaimed himself to be the long awaited Jewish Messiah. His followers were many, including the famous Rabbi Akiba.[9] The Jewish Christians could not participate in the rebellion because of Bar Cochba's messianic claims. For the Jewish Christians, Jesus alone was the Messiah. The Christians left Palestine for Antioch and Alexandria, where there were already large numbers of Jewish and Gentile Christians.

The Bar Cochba rebellion ended in the complete extinction of the Palestinian Jews. Each day thousands of Jews were executed by the Romans. The people disappeared from the land.

Antioch and Alexandria were great hellenic intellectual centers. Under the influence of Greek thinkers, the Christian interpretation of the New Testament fell more and more into Greek language and categories. The precise relationship of Jesus to Yahweh became a question of major concern. The Antiochian school was more conservative in their interpretation. They opted for a literal understanding of the New Testament, trying to remain faithful to the original text. The Alexandrian school was much more liberal in their biblical interpretation. They opted for the allegorical interpretation of the texts.

Eventually the different approaches split into political as well as religious factions and the stage was set for the battle of the First Council of Nicea. Arius and Athanasius personified the struggle. Arius, following the tradition of the Synoptics, concluded that the relationship of Jesus to God was that of the greatest of the prophets. Jesus was God's revelation to man, but only as a man.[10] Athanasius, speaking for the "orthodox" held to the divinity of Jesus. Jesus was true God and true Man, and his divinity was of the same substance as that of the Father. The lines were drawn. And Christianity was irrevocably divided. This initial split would later be translated into the division between the East and West. Perhaps, the fundamental scandal of Christianity can be grounded in the Council of Nicea which took onto itself the prerogative of clothing in human language once and for all the definitive description of the relationship of

Jesus to God. Nicea solved nothing. Today, the question continues to be asked by many Christians and the answers are equally divisive.

There can be little doubt that St. John and St. Paul refer to the relationship of Jesus to God in terms of Divine Sonship.[11] In the development of theological interpretation this divine relationship found clarification in the framework of Hypostatic Union, the union of two natures in one hypostasis or person. Christian theology spoke about the unity of the divine nature with the human nature of Jesus in the second person of the Trinity. The result of this unity did not destroy the integrity of the human nature of Jesus. Both the divine nature of the Second Person and human nature of Jesus retained their identity and their proper activity.

From this philosophical explanation of the relationship of Jesus to God it was concluded that the one person, Jesus, had two distinct natures, one human, one divine. Each one of these natures had its own proper expression. The unity of the two natures did not in any way reduce the humanness of Jesus. Through his human nature, Jesus as man truly suffered the agony of crucifixion. God did not die, the human Jesus did. However, because the nature of Jesus was assumed by the Second Person of the Trinity, the total person of Jesus is called the Divine Son of God. His unique relation to God in terms of his divine sonship was due to the assumption of human nature by the Second Person who in the context of the Trinity is Son of God the Father. Because the Son of God became man, the human nature he assumed also became the Son of God. We are not speaking of a total absorption of the human into the divine, but rather the unique relation existing between the human nature and the divine because of the divine assumption of that nature. This human nature raised to divine sonship is what Jesus wished to share with all men.

Grace can be described in many ways. In the final analysis, it is the activity of God upon man. The Hypostatic Union is just such a grace. The gracious activity of the Son of God assumes a human nature. The Incarnation, then, is the gracious movements of God uniting the human nature of man with the divine nature in the person historically known as Jesus Christ.

The above vocabulary used in describing the Incarnation as Hypostatic Union is a vocabulary that flows out of Greek philosophical categories. These categories were used by Greek Christian thinkers to clarify for their times the relationship of Jesus to Yahweh. These categories did offer and continue to offer powerful insights into the Christian understanding or interpretation of Jesus. The question, however, is, "Are they the *only* possible categories in which to express the meaning of Jesus?" There is a large segment of Christianity that would answer yes. But from our point of view, human language will remain essentially inadequate to communicate religious mysteries in a definitive form.

Language is the tool of social and cultural communication.[12] Culture and society are constantly changing. What were adequate and helpful tools of communicating the mystery of Jesus to the Greek Christians or to the later feudalistic world may very well be inadequate communication of religious truth today. The fundamental crisis of Christianity today is one of archaic and incommunicable theological language.[13] The only people who would really be comfortable with the above vocabulary used in describing the Incarnation in terms of the Hypostatic Union would be those familiar with scholastic terminology. The fact that these language tools can no longer communicate adequately is verifiable among the younger generation of Christians who find such expressions as Trinity, Nature, Person, Hypostatic Union, Grace and Incarnation as incomprehensible jargon compared to their own linguistic tools. The process of evolving generations and evolving language tools of communication cannot be impeded. The communication gap continues to expand so long as structured churches insist on clothing their religious truths in meaningless ancient language.

THE RELATIONSHIP OF JESUS TO GOD: A Modern Myth

How then can we re-express the relationship of Jesus to God? The consubstantiality of the Nicene Creed was one way of expressing it. The Hypostatic Union of the Thomists was another way. Both were meaningful insights into the mystery of this relationship. The following effort to re-express these insights does not imply a rejection of them, but a building upon them in terms perhaps more relevant to the culture in which we find ourselves. But then, in the last analysis, this effort too will need to be recast by later generations.

In the creation of the world, the creative act of God can be described as the first Incarnation, the total unity of God with the matter he created. At every step in the process of evolution God is present. The initial created world stuff possessed a twofold characteristic; an inner driving force or psychism and an exterior structure or complexity. The inner driving force of the primitive particles of matter reached out and sought unity with other particles to form ever more complex structures and consequently, ever more intensely conscious aspects of matter.

As the complexity increased, so did the psychism.[14] Evolution of matter then also implies the evolution of thought. In this sense the creative act of God as an ongoing process is what we mean by evolution. As matter evolved into ever more complex and conscious forms, God's involvement intensified. God's relation to the matter he initially created reached a dramatic highpoint in the God-man unity we know as Jesus Christ. The unity of God and man in Jesus takes place at a higher level of the organization and consciousness of matter, but is a further extension of the unity of God with the matter he initially created. The point is not to separate the two incarnations but see God-becoming-man as an evolution of God-becoming-matter within a linear and historical process. It is in this context that we call God's first creative act the First Incarnation and the creative act of unity with Jesus as the Second Incarnation. In neither case does matter become divine, but matter is united to God and therefore, enjoys a unique relationship to God. Primitive matter was a primitive expression of that relationship. Jesus was a climactic expression of that relationship, the response of self-reflective matter (man) to the personal call of God.

This is not Pantheism. It is not pantheistic to speak of all creation as evolving from one level of expression to another in unity with the divine. It is no more pantheistic to speak of the initial creative act as First Incarnation than to speak of the unity of God with man in Jesus as the Second Incarnation. What we wish to establish is the continuity between the unity of God with all his creation and the personification of that unity in time in the human being of Jesus. Consequently, throughout all levels of evolution, beginning with creation itself, matter was evolving to that time when Jesus would preach to man that their true nature consisted in their relation of sonship to God. But, intelligent matter, in its struggle for self-awareness slowly arrived at an understanding that authentic human existence was grounded in sonship to God. This was the most powerful insight of Jesus. He claimed to be the unique Son of God. And indeed he was. But he willed to share this sonship with his fellow men. His preaching of man's sonship to God has yet to reach the ears of the community of men. If we are truly sons of God, we are then as particles of intelligent matter bound together in an intimate relationship that far exceeds our primitive understanding of the word "brother."

In the linear process of the evolution of matter man comes forth as the most exteriorly complex and interiorly conscious expression of matter. Man is highly organized matter capable of self-reflection. Yet, he is not free from the limitations of created matter. Man's exterior complexity remains subject to the basic problem of all compositions . . . decomposition. Sickness, disease, accident, death still are very much a part of his biological makeup. Matter gropes to overcome these threats to existence. Man's consciousness, like his complexity, is also subject to groping limitations. Hatred, anger, jealousy, misunderstanding, fear, doubt, still are a part of man's stumbling search for self-meaning. The world of man moving toward unity is blocked time and time again by the evil within the human consciousness.

Yet, historically, human consciousness has come a long way. It has not reached its end. But the search for meaning, brutal as it has been, continues to open to man the understanding of what it means to be human. The basic and most common element in the conscious struggle for unity is love. Love is the inner driving force of human consciousness reaching out toward ever more complex forms of unity. Primitive man has grown from the brutal individual to family to clan to tribe to nation to internationalist. Man is young. He is still primitive. Unities such as cities, states, countries, nations, and internations have evolved, but not much beyond the level of primitive. Families, cities, countries and nations still explode into limitations of consciousness; hatred, anger, and war. These limitations could bring about the abortion of man as a relatively new species of life upon earth. One nuclear war would do the trick.

There is a hope within mankind that man's biological aggressiveness will give way to the inner driving force of love. The hope is based on a happening within the total organism of mankind. This happening was Jesus. Jesus, like all men, was a particle of intelligent matter. His self-awareness, like that of Abraham and Moses, focused on his relationship to God. Jesus understood like no other man understood that God is truly father of the man. God communicated himself to Jesus and through this self-communication established Jesus as God's revelation to man concerning authentic human existence.

From this time on, human existence would be understood in terms of the divine sonship of man. Jesus came forth in the process of evolution as *that* particle of self-reflective matter in whom God revealed His divine unity with created man. The incarnation of man's world and God's kingdom became personalized and objectified through Jesus. This is redemption. Jesus gave to man a whole new thrust toward God. Through Jesus, man began to become aware of his sonship with God. Through Jesus, man began to understand the pervading presence of the divine within matter. Through Jesus, the inner driving force of human consciousness began to be spelled out in terms of love. The redemptive value of Jesus was not a buying back from the forces of evil. It was not a payment for original sin, especially in view of the contemporary re-expression of original sin. It was the preaching of the sonship of man to God and the preaching of love as the inner driving force of human unity that gave mankind a chance for survival.

Through Jesus, God revealed Himself in a new era of human history. The unity of the divinity with mankind in the person of Jesus would initiate an intense struggle within man to overcome the limitations of the human consciousness. These limitations are grounded deeply within the human psyche. The conflict between the inner driving force of love and the divisive alienating force of hate are still very much a part of the human experience. Yet, through the happening of Jesus the hope is that in the process of evolution the inner driving force of love will overcome the biological aggressiveness of man, resulting in the ultimate unity of all the particles of human intelligence into a unified organism deeply aware of its unity with the divinity.

CONCLUSION

The relationship of Jesus to God remains a mystery and for that reason it is unique. Within the framework of evolution our description of that relationship is grounded in the man Jesus through whose self-awareness God revealed or communicated to man that basic union with the divine envisioned at the moment of creation. Jesus remains the unique symbol of that union because in the process of evolution it is he who is singled out as the vehicle of God's revelation. In this self-communication of God prismed through Jesus the meaning of human love comes through as a necessary binding force of mankind's unity with itself and with God.

The meaning of salvation is unity with God. The essential element of the Jesus kerygma is love of God, love of self, love of fellow men. The primacy of love as the driving force of human consciousness has been irrevocably established by God's self-communication through Jesus. But within the process of evolution the ideal of Christian human love is undergoing a painful and slow growth. Christianity is still in its infancy. Infant Christianity still stumbles and gropes in its effort to achieve that measure of love revealed to it through the life and meaning of Jesus. The two world wars were primarily wars of Christians, a standing indictment of its infantilism. But the hope remains that the human spirit of Jesus, which like God Himself, pervades the community of man will direct man in the struggle against his destructive aggressiveness and competition. The threat of atomic extinction or suffocation through technological competition can be overcome to the extent that cooperative effort grows within the inner driving force of human love.

The Christian *pessimism* is that man's basic animal instinct, his biological aggression and competition will end in the extinction of the species. A possibility to be acknowledged. The Christian *optimism* is that under the influence of the pervasive presence of the spirit of Jesus, man will overcome his destructive aggression and competition and turn his energies toward building up the community of man toward ever greater levels of unity. The redemptive direction of Jesus will continue the thrust of man in the process of evolution until mankind has reached that level of unified complexity and intense consciousness that will set the stage for a whole new leap into a new experience of God.

QUESTIONS FOR DISCUSSION

1. What is the historical relationship between the Babylonian Son of Man and the Greek Anthropos?

2. Were the Babylonian Son of Man and the Hebrew Messiah ever identified in Hebrew literature?

3. What is meant by the Hypostatic Union?

4. Can the relationship of Jesus to God be expressed in ways other than the Hypostatic Union?

5. What is the relationship between the first and the second incarnation?

6. What does the Redemption by Jesus mean?

BIBLIOGRAPHICAL REFERENCES

CHAPTER SEVEN: THE RELATION OF GOD
TO THE MAN JESUS

1. Brown, Raymond. *Jesus God and Man*. Milwaukee: The Bruce Publishing Co., 1967, p. 1.

2. Van Buren, Paul. *The Secular Meaning of The Gospel*. New York: Macmillan, 1963, pp. 159-171.

3. Brown. *op. cit.*, pp. 23-28.

4. Mowinkel, Sigmund. *He That Cometh*. New York: Abington Press, 1954, p. 421.

5. *Ibid.*, p. 429.

6. *Ibid.*, p. 427.

7. *Ibid.*, p. 421.

8. Schnackenburg, Rudolf. *The Gospel According to St. John*. New York: 1968, p. 124.

9. Shurer, Emil. *The Jewish People in the Time of Jesus*. New York: Schocken Books, 1963, p. 300.

10. Van Buren. *op. cit.*, p. 28.

11. Brown. *op. cit.*, pp. 23-28.

12. Macquarrie, John. *God Talk*. New York: Harper & Row, 1967, p. 78.

13. Dewart, Leslie. *The Future of Belief*. New York: Herder and Herder, 1966, p. 108-109.

14. Teilhard de Chardin, Pierre. *The Phenomenon of Man*. New York: Harper Torchbooks, 1959, pp. 298-301.

8. The Resurrection to Afterlife

the experience of death as the basis of religion · the Egyptian afterlife · the Babylonian-Hebrew afterlife · Christian afterlife · bodiless resurrection · organized centers of consciousness

At one time or other man is confronted with the mysterious phenomenon of death. Conclusions from this confrontation are clothed either in the language of afterlife or complete annihilation. Some anthropologists understand the afterlife as a self-projection on the part of man in the face of death. The question of the afterlife is like the question of God. The answers to these questions are buried deep within the personality of the human being whose life stance either affirms or rejects the existence of an afterlife. We can prove the existence of an afterlife no more than we can prove the existence of God. Both are faith-assumptions. Both assumptions are personal intuitions which flow out of the life-experience of the individual in search for self-meaning.

126

The life stance of the atheist also represents the personal conviction of one whose search for meanings ends with a different conclusion. Believers load their case against the non-believer by invoking some special grace, or gift, or enlightenment, or selectivity grounded in the activity of God. The arrogance of Christianity is obvious on this point. On the other hand, the non-believer loads the case against the believer by saying that God is a crutch, a Linus blanket, for one who cannot get through life without such addenda. Respect for personal human conviction is passed over in favor of irrational rational arguments for or against the existence of God and of an afterlife.

Christians believe in the existence of God. They also believe in the afterlife in light of their sonship to the Father, revealed in Jesus. This sonship which Jesus preached is an eternal sonship, a leap far beyond the *sheol* concept of Judaism. Resurrection to afterlife is a fundamental belief of contemporary Christianity. Yet, this belief is clothed in mythological language of very ancient times. Our concern with Resurrection to Afterlife is not by way of rejection of this belief but to find language forms more viable than our inherited mythologies.

Primitive myths of Resurrection to Afterlife are intimately related to the origins of religious belief. The first evidence of religious belief is that of the burial rights of Neanderthal. Neanderthal buried his dead in a unique way. The dead were buried with provisions, food, and hunting weapons.[1] The spirits of the dead gradually were venerated as ancestral spirits. In India the primitive Bavondas believed that the spirits of their ancestors inhabited the mountains, the streams, the rivers, the lakes, the forests, and the trees.[2]

Death itself, like all the phenomena of nature, was a revelatory event, out of which man drew religious meaning. The question is which came first, belief in gods or belief in the afterlife? The question is all but impossible to answer because of the lack of records. Yet, the possibility remans that God initiated his self-communication to man in man's experience of death. Out of man's reflection upon death, God led man slowly to faith in the eternal divine life.

THE EGYPTIAN AFTERLIFE

One of the most elaborate theologies of death was developed by the ancient Egyptians. At first, only the kings enjoyed the prerogative of an afterlife, most likely because of their intimate and privileged relationship to the gods. Gradually it was understood that even the commoner could partake in the afterlife. The Egyptians believed in a birdlike spirit or soul deep within man which after death flew out of the body. The tombs of the dead had openings to permit the "birds" to escape. The spirit, however, loved the body and longed to be reunited to it. The spirit could not be happy until it finally came to rest within the body. This was the underlying reason for the Egyptian effort to preserve the bodies of the dead by mummification. This explanation of the longing of union between spirit and body is not far removed from the later Thomistic teaching concerning the violent state of the departed soul awaiting unity with the body at the final resurrection.

The Egyptian idea of the state of the afterlife was very rich. The departed spirits became stars finally to merge with the great sun-god. In some cases perilous journeys across treacherous sky-seas were required before the spirit could reach a resting place near the sun. Another tradition speaks of the valley of Osiris; a far off land of pleasure and plenty. In the Egyptian Book of the Dead the ritual describes the spirit as standing before a judge listing all the evil he did not do. The list comprised such things as murder, adultery, injustice, stealing—a list similar to but older than the Hebrew Ten Commandments. After recording all the evil things the spirit did not do, the judge then began a list of the good deeds performed by the spirit. He was judged as worthy of entering a certain level of the Kingdom of Osiris, depending on his accomplishments. If he were judged unworthy to enter, he was cast into a fiery hell.[3]

THE BABYLONIAN AND HEBREW AFTERLIFE

Egypt, unlike Israel and Babylonia, enjoyed a history of relative calm. It stretched along the Nile, nestled between the mysterious deserts. From long before Abraham to Jesus, Egypt was a quiet land free from the major migrations and invasions that afflicted Israel and Babylonia. Egypt enjoyed the leisure time to reflect upon death and to develop and elaborate theology of the afterlife. Israel and Babylonia were much more concerned with the struggle for surviving the present life and this left little time to worry about the afterlife. Life between the Tigris and Euphrates was in constant political upheaval. One invasion after another patterned the waves of the sea. Life was snatched in the short calm of the troughs. The energies of self-reflection for the Babylonians were spent on life, not death. They believed in a land-of-no-return to where all dead went. It was a joyless place of repose, a sort of final resting place. The land-of-no-return is not itself described but simply stated.[4]

In this statement of the afterlife by the Babylonians we have basically the *sheol* concept of the Hebrews. *Sheol*, like the land-of-no-return, was a joyless place.[5] The Hebrews like the Babylonians, were preoccupied with survival. Life was far more problematic than death. The Hebrews did improve somewhat upon the Babylonian afterlife in that the Hebrews understood their own life to continue in some way through their children. In later Judaism under the Greek influence, questions concerning resurrection and afterlife began to take shape.

CHRISTIAN RESURRECTION AND THE AFTERLIFE

Within Christian tradition belief in the Resurrection of Jesus as the prototype of the Resurrection of man is an essential faith-conviction. The Resurrection of Jesus is described in all four New Testament Gospels and forms a key theme in the Letters of St. Paul. However, the Resurrection of Jesus in the New Testament is clothed in the mythological language frameworks of the times.[6] The Resurrection of Jesus is not an original myth. Men spoke of resurrection long before the interpreters of Jesus. By speaking of the Resurrection of Jesus as myth we remind the reader of the mythological language of the New Testament and suggest that the reality of the

Christ-Resurrection is clothed in the Babylonian resurrection of the Son of Man filtered through the Greek Anthropos myth, Hebrewized in the Apocalyptic Wisdom literature.[7]

Besides the many resurrection myths existing at the time of Jesus, there is the mythological language peculiar to the New Testament. In the four Gospels the account of the Resurrection of Jesus is clothed in symbols. In each account there are many proverbial angels —manifestations of the divine presence or activity. Light, another symbol of the divine, also is present in the four resurrection narratives. Matthew places the resurrection scene late at night with the lightening face of an angel piercing the darkness (Mt 28:1-4). Matthew also repeats his death earthquake with a resurrection earthquake, a symbol of the shattering presence of the divine. Mark and Luke place the resurrection at dawn when the sun has just risen. The symbol of light of the rising sun coupled with the dazzling whiteness of the angel raiment pervade the whole scene with divine power and presence (Mk 16:2-6; Lk 24:2-5). In John, the angels, dressed in whiteness, speak to Mary Magdalene (Jn 20:11-13).

Symbolism points to the reality beyond itself. The symbolism of the resurrection narrative points to a deeper reality than the empty tomb. However, later Christianity confused the symbolism with the reality of historical fact. The meaning of the Resurrection of Jesus became caught up in an overemphasis on the empty tomb and the resurrected physical body.

Recent understanding of the mythological language of the New Testament places strain on the traditional

Christian interpretation of the resurrection of the physical body. This preoccupation with the physical resurrection was further strengthened by the Aristotelian description of man as a composite of body and soul (matter and form). The resurrection of Jesus came to be understood as a reunity of body and soul. Physical resurrection was considered a prototype for the resurrection of man with the insistence that final resurrection consists in the reunion of all dead spirits with their earthly body in some way spiritualized at the final judgment. There are, however, two major difficulties with this traditional view. Firstly, there is our human experience, which indicates what process of decomposition the human body goes through until it is reduced to its basic chemical elements. It strains human intelligence to insist that final resurrection must imply a unity with our same earthly body. This is not a biblical problem. It is a philosophical problem which has been traditionally resolved in favor of Aristotle's physical description of the essence of man. Secondly, biblical research shows us the profound danger and the profound ignorance involved in the elevation of symbol to the level of historical fact.

THE CONTEMPORARY PROBLEM

There are two extreme positions in regard to an understanding of the Resurrection of Jesus. The traditional understanding is found in the creeds of Christianity insisting on belief in the resurrection of the physical body. In 1274, the Council of Lyons reiterates the creeds, "The third day He arose by a true resurrection of the body."[8]

The other extreme position is that initiated by Rudolf Bultmann but carried to a logical conclusion by Paul Van Buren. Bultmann sees the Cross and the Resurrection as one cosmic event. For Bultmann, the meaning of the Resurrection, like the meaning of the Cross, is that of an eschatological event in which contemporary man can participate through existential faith. Bultmann does not deny that something happened on Easter Sunday.[9] The question is not whether something happened but to whom. Bultmann's answer would focus on the apostles and disciples in whom faith in Jesus took on an insightful meaning. Bultmann's answer concerning the historicity of the resurrection can be summed up in his words, "An historical fact which involves a resurrection from the dead is utterly inconceivable."[10] For Bultmann the resurrection is the faith-experience of Jesus by the apostolic community, not the empty tomb.

Paul Van Buren pushes Bultmann a little further. The resurrection is the psychological event of the apostles and disciples of Jesus as they gradually come to share the sense of freedom so much a part of Jesus. Van Buren sums up his position in the following words, "The man who says Jesus is Lord is saying that the history of Jesus and what happened to him on Easter has exercised a liberating effect on him. . . ."[11]

An Alternative to the Extremes

We are indebted to Rudolf Bultmann for pointing out to us the mythological language framework of the New Testament resurrection narratives. In view of this he rightly distinguishes the symbols from historical fact.

Traditional Christianity has insisted on accepting the resurrection narrative literally. Consequently, the resurrection of the physical body is integral not only to the resurrection of Jesus but to that of man at the final judgment. It is St. Paul who hints at a possible solution to these extremes. Whenever Paul refers to the resurrected body of Jesus, he qualifies the body with the descriptive "pneumata" (spiritualized).[12] Paul, like the other disciples, wanted to communicate to his readers his faith experience of the continued presence of the human Jesus within the community and within the cosmos. His monolithic concept of man was that of an animated-body-person. It would be inconceivable to speak of the man Jesus without in some way speaking of the body. Paul speaks of the body of Jesus but with the most important qualification of "spiritualized."

The apostolic community, including Paul, preached the continuing presence of Jesus in the mythology of the Resurrection of the third day, the light and darkness theme, the divine presence through angels, the divine power through earthquake. From this point of view, the resurrection narratives are mythological or symbolic narratives pointing to the reality of the faith-conviction that Jesus continues to exist within the community of man.

However, consistent with our previous consideration of the continuity of human existence we add the following. Accepting the mythological description of resurrection as pointed out by Bultmann and Van Buren, we do not accept their conclusion that the only thing that happened on Easter was a psychological experience on the part of the apostolic community. The Resurrection of Jesus was, for Jesus, a leap into a new level of human existence. The human consciousness of Jesus continued in existence after death as a particle of personal and organized intelligence, capable of moving and acting upon the cosmos out of which he came. This particle of spiritualized matter leaped to a level of conscious existence with God but with an intense relationship with the community of man and the community of matter. This description would be consistent with St. Paul's cosmic texts concerning Christ (Col 1:17, 2:10, 3:11; Eph 4:9).

This new level of human existence of Jesus in union with God was revealed to man by Jesus through the many physical manifestations of himself after death. As an individual and organized particle of intelligence, Jesus, because of his unique relationship with the Father, could and did manifest himself to the community of man by converting matter, energy, space, and time into a physical extension of his psychic self. The many manifestations of Jesus to his disciples were real physical expressions of his human consciousness communicating his continued existence and presence to the community of man. The resurrection of Jesus cannot be limited to the physical body and the empty tomb, nor be a more psychological experience of faith on the part of his immediate followers. Their faith was grounded on the revelation of Jesus to them through the many physical manifestations reported in the New Testament. Jesus achieved a new level of psychic existence in union with the Father which through his resurrectional manifestations, he willed to share with man. The mythological language of the gospels was the viable language tool of the community witnessing to the manifestations of Jesus.

These appearances truly pointed to a resurrection as a leap into a new psychic existence to be shared by all mankind and revealed through the person of Jesus.

Jesus continues to be the unique son of God who revealed man's sonship and God's fatherhood. The spirit or human psyche of Jesus remains active and operative within the community of man today. Where God is, Jesus is. Like the God of Tillich, Jesus is present as the depth and ground of our being. Like the omega point of Teilhard de Chardin, the psychic energy of Jesus remains buried deeply within the cosmic forces of evolution, continuing the thrust of mankind toward a more intense unity with God.

Jesus then is truly the prototype of our resurrection. Our existence after death will be like that of Jesus. Our human consciousness will be present within the cosmos in unity with the human consciousness of Jesus and in unity with God. A concept of the resurrection of the body no longer makes sense in terms of the Aristotelian description of man as a composite of body and soul. We know from our human experience what happens to the body after death. It literally crumbles into many diverse chemical molecules. In a very real sense we are dust and to dust we return. When the resurrection is described as a reunion of the body and the soul at the time of final judgment the Christian belief of eternal sonship becomes bogged down in an ancient description of man. When at death the human consciousness leaps to a new level of existence, the relationship to a specific body is irrevocably lost. Both in terms of the body, which is reduced to the elements of the cosmos, and in terms of the human consciousness, which is in union with God, man has a whole new relationship to the cosmos from which he came. The description of man as a composite of body and soul is one of the many ways to describe man. From our point of view, man is not a dichotomy of body and soul. He is a total unit of energy manifested through the inner energy of psychism and the exterior energy of structure. There is of course an intimate relationship between the two expressions of energy. But at death the psychic energy leaps free of the exterior structured body. Even during our earthly existence our consciousness is a type of constant conversion of matter into energy of thought. This is not a strange concept when the history of evolution itself signifies a leap of lesser forms of consciousness-complexity to the highest complex-conscious form of man.

Self reflection represents a whole new level of existence for the interior psychic energy of matter. Death, in a similar way, represents a leap to a whole new level of existence. From the point of view of a Christian believer this leap results in the unity of the human consciousness with God. Man then, from this point of view, is *not* a composite of body and soul. He is an element of matter constantly undergoing psychic change. Consciousness itself is as much an element of evolution as are material structures. Death then is a transformation of the human consciousness from one form of existence to another. The new state of existence like that of Christ, is united to God and like God, pervades the entire cosmos. The only relationship that the human consciousness has to the human body is in terms of the reduction of the human body into cosmic dust. The state of the afterlife then is a new level of existence on a dramatically higher level of organized consciousness. Means of communication between those existing on this level would be different from the means of communication used within the community of man on earth. Consequently, little or no communication passes between the two levels of existence. Perhaps though, in the phenomena of extra-sensory-perception, breakthroughs of communication have been made.

What Then of Hell?

So far the description of the afterlife has been in terms of the unity of human psyches with God. First of all, it would be helpful to consider the judgment of Jesus and the resurrection as one event at the instant of death. There is ultimately no reason to separate the two in time categories. Out of the framework of body and soul Christian tradition has separated the judgment of man by Jesus at the moment of death from resurrection or glorification. If one is found wanting in his relationship to Jesus as brother and to God as son, whatever purgation required would be a purgation of intensity rather than duration. The human consciousness then at the moment of death is either found fit or made fit for the new level of existence in unity with God.

But what about a person who has lived consistently a life of evil, one whose influence during life was more destructive of the community of man rather than constructive? Destructive living implies some degree of alienation from one's fellow men. An evil man is one who has alienated himself from men and consequently from God. In this state of alienation he is isolated from the community. Loneliness, guilt, hatred build up within the alienated man. To the extent that one has lived a life of alienation, his relationship to God in the afterlife will be one of alienation. He will continue to feel his isolation and his hatred.

I cannot suggest an answer to the question of the eternity of hell or state of alienation. The eternity of hell as often held by Christians, flows out of the Greek convictions of the changelessness of reality. From an evolutionary point of view the state of alienation in the afterlife could change to the extent that the human consciousness seeks to correct its alienation with some expressions of love. The isolation of the individual conscience from the evolving totality of mankind could be a temporal state of the evil consciousness until the person began to seek total unity with man and with God. The human consciousness of the afterlife continues its human operations of knowing and loving. In unity with God in the afterlife the conscious energy of knowing and loving is enriched. In the situation of the evil human consciousness, the sense of alienation is intensified. The person then may at any time begin to seek that unity which from the very beginning of creation has been the inner driving force of all energy. The changelessness of hell does not seem to be consistent with the overview of evolution. Ultimately, the changelessness of the state of alienation or the possibility of change will be expressions of religious belief.

QUESTIONS FOR DISCUSSION

1. Is there an afterlife?

2. Why were the Egyptian and the Hebrew views of after-life so different?

3. What is the basis for the description of man as a composite of body and soul?

4. Is the resurrection of the body a necessary element of Christian faith?

5. What is meant by a new level of consciousness?

6. Is there a hell?

BIBLIOGRAPHICAL REFERENCES

CHAPTER EIGHT: THE RESURRECTION
TO AFTERLIFE

1. Noss, John, B. *Man's Religions.* New York: Macmillan, 1963, p. 5.

2. *Ibid.,* p. 48.

3. *Ibid.,* pp. 59-73.

4. *Ibid.,* p. 73.

5. DeVaux, Roland. *Ancient Israel, Its Life and Institutions.* London: Darton, Longman and Todd, 1962, p. 56.

6. Bultmann, Rudolf. *Kerygma and Myth.* New York: Harper Torchbooks, 1966, pp. 38-43.

7. Schnackenburg, Rudolf. *The Gospel According to John.* New York: Herder and Herder, 1968, pp. 543-557.

8. *The Church Teaches.* ed., John F. Clarkson, et al., St. Louis: B. Herder Book Co., 1960, p. 141.

9. Bultmann, Rudolf. *op. cit.,* p. 111.

10. *Ibid.,* p. 39.

11. Van Buren, Paul. *The Secular Meaning of the Gospel.* New York: Macmillan, 1966, p. 141.

12. Cerfaux, Lucien. *Christ in the Theology of St. Paul.* New York: Herder and Herder, 1959, p. 78.